A TEXAS BLUEBONNET:
LADY BIRD JOHNSON

(A VOLUME IN THE PRESIDENTIAL WIVES SERIES)

OTHER BOOKS IN THE PRESIDENTIAL WIVES SERIES

Robert P. Watson
Series Editor

Dolley Madison
Paul M. Zall
2001. ISBN 1-56072-930-9. (Hardcover)
2001. ISBN 1-56072-937-6. (Softcover)

A "Bully" First Lady: Edith Kermit Roosevelt
Tom Lansford
2001. ISBN 1-59033-086-2. (Hardcover)
2003. ISBN 1-56072-648-8. (Softcover)

Sarah Childress Polk, First Lady of Tennessee and Washington
Barbara Bennett Peterson
2002. ISBN 1-59033-145-1. (Hardcover)
2002. ISBN 1-56072-551-1. (Softcover)

Frances Clara Folsom Cleveland
Stephen F. Robar
2002. ISBN 1-59033-245-8. (Hardcover)
2004. ISBN 1-59454-150-7 (Softcover)

Lucretia
John Shaw
2002. ISBN 1-59033-349-7. (Hardcover)
2004. ISBN 1-59454-151-5 (Softcover)

Jackie Kennedy: Images and Reality
Mohammed Badrul Alam
2003. ISBN 1-59033-366-7.

Betty Ford: A Symbol of Strength
Jeffrey S. Ashley
2003. ISBN 1-59033-407-8(Hardcover)
2004. ISBN 1-59454-149-3 (Softcover)

Nancy Reagan: The Woman Behind the Man
Pierre-Marie Loizeau
2004. ISBN 1-59033-759-X.

Dutiful Service : The Life of Mrs. Mamie Eisenhower
Robert E. Dewhirst
2004. ISBN 1-59454-007-1.

Ellen A. Wilson: The Woman Who Made a President
Sina Dubovoy
2004. ISBN 1-59033-791-3.

Eliza Johnson: Unknown First Lady
Jean Choate
2004. ISBN 1-59454-097-7

Grace Coolidge: Sudden Star
Cynthia D. Bittinger
2005. ISBN 1-59454-473-5

Lucy Webb Hayes:
A First Lady by Example
Russell L. Mahan
2005. ISBN 1-59454-011-X

A TEXAS BLUEBONNET: LADY BIRD JOHNSON

David Murphy

Nova History Publications, Inc.
New York

For permission to use material from this book please contact us:
Telephone 631-231-7269; Fax 631-231-8175
Web Site: http://www.novapublishers.com

NOTICE TO THE READER

Library of Congress Cataloging-in-Publication Data
Murphy, David.
Texas bluebonnet : Lady Bird Johnson / David Murphy.
        p. cm.
Includes bibliographical references and index.
ISBN 1-59454-556-1
1. Johnson, Lady Bird, 1912- 2. Presidents' spouses--United States--Biography. I. Title.
E848.J64M87   2005
973.923'092--dc22   2005017108

Published by Nova History Publications,
New York

*Dedicated in loving memory to my
late grandfather, Marshall T. Presley*

CONTENTS

FOREWORD

Robert P. Watson

The old saying that "behind every successful man is a woman" is perhaps nowhere more evident than in the White House. Even a cursory examination of the wives of presidents reveals a group of remarkable individuals who made many contributions to the lives and careers of their husbands, the presidency, and even the nation. Over the course of U.S. history first ladies have presided over state dinners, overseen extensive historical renovations of the Executive Mansion, held press conferences, campaigned for their husbands, testified before Congress, championed important social causes, and addressed the United Nations.

As a candidate for the presidency speaking of the role his wife would assume in his administration Bill Clinton stated that when the public elects a president, they are getting "two for the price of one!" To an extent such a statement has always been true. First ladies have been a viable part of the presidency since the nation's founding. Of the men who served as president during the country's history, nearly all of them served with a first lady at their side. Only a handful of presidents have held the office without their spouses. For instance, both Andrew Jackson and Chester A. Arthur had lost their wives prior to their presidencies; Rachel Jackson dying in the interim between her husband's election and his inauguration and Ellen Arthur just prior to her husband's Vice Presidency. The wives of both Thomas Jefferson and Martin Van Buren passed away years before their presidencies. But they were exceptions. Only two bachelor presidents have been elected, Grover Cleveland and James Buchanan, however the former married while in office. Three presidential wives died while serving in the White House:

Letitia Tyler, Caroline Harrison, and Ellen Wilson. However, both President John Tyler and President Woodrow Wilson later remarried while in office.

Presidential wives have served without pay and, until very recently, often without proper recognition. So too have they wielded political power and social influence despite the fact that they are neither elected nor appointed. In part because they are not elected or accountable to the citizenry and in part because of strict social conventions that precluded women from participating in politics for much of the nation's history, presidential wives have been forced to exercise their power and influence in a behind-the-scenes manner. Yet, in this capacity many wives have functioned as their husband's trusted confidante and private political advisor.

Presidential wives have faced great challenges, not the least of which include the loss of privacy and specter of assassination looming for themselves and their families. The presidency is arguably the most demanding job in the country and the challenges of the office are experienced by the president's family. Amazingly, several first ladies served while trying to raise a family. Presidential wives have faced severe scrutiny, an invasive press corps and curious public, and criticism from journalists and the president's political enemies. This is perhaps one of the experiences that all first ladies have shared. Not even popular wives like Martha Washington, Abigail Adams, or Jacqueline Kennedy were spared from harsh personal attacks.

The first ladyship has been the "unknown institution" of the White House. For most of its history it has been ignored by scholars and overlooked by those studying national and presidential politics. However, this is slowly changing. The public, press, and scholars are beginning to take note of the centrality of the first lady to the presidency. A new view of the president's spouse as a "partner" in the presidency is replacing more traditional views of presidential wives. Even though the Founding Fathers of the country gave no thought to the president's wife and the Constitution is silent concerning her duties, today the "office" has become a powerful, recognized institution within the presidency, complete with staff and budgetary resources that rival the so-called "key" presidential advisors.

It is also an intriguing office whose occupants are no less fascinating themselves. Indeed, the presidential wives are a diverse lot that includes new brides barely out of their teens to grandmothers who had spent a lifetime married to men that would become president. There have been women of refinement and wealth and there have been wives who would seem ill-prepared for the challenges of the White House. And of course, there have been successes and there have been failures.

The first ladyship is one of the nation's most challenging and dynamic public offices. So too is it an office still in development. In the words of First Lady Barbara Bush, concluding her remarks when delivering the commencement speech at Wellesley College, "And who knows? Somewhere out in this audience may even be someone who will one day follow in my footsteps, and preside over the White House as the President's spouse. I wish *him* well!"

In the volumes of this Series the reader will find the stories of women who fashioned the course of American history. It is the goal of the publishers and myself that this book and each volume in the Presidential Wives Series shed light on this important office and reveal the lives of the women behind the American presidency.

I hope you enjoy this book and the entire Series!

Robert P. Watson, Series Editor

ACKNOWLEDGEMENTS

I would be remiss if I didn't begin by thanking all of those who have helped me and inspired me as I worked on this, my first book. First of all, I would like to thank my loving parents, Mack and Annette Murphy who never gave up faith in me throughout this entire project and my brother, Marshall Tyler, for his help and support My sister, Shelli Murphy provided much supported much needed morale. Also, I wish to thank my grandmother, Geneva Presley, for her support to me. I would like thank other members of my family for the encouragement, my aunts Rita, Brenda, Robin, and Janet and my uncles, John, Larry, and Rick. Also, I wish to thank the members of the vast Murphy family for their support, particularly my grandmother, Mary Murphy. I also wish to thank my friends Ben Carter, Billy Parker, Jason Tackett, Ryan Igbanol, Carla Owens, Wanda Gaines, Chris Aldridge, Rev. Jana Hall, and my fraternity brothers from Delta Tau Delta for their support and encouragement.

I extend my sincere appreciation to my editor, Professor Robert P. Watson of the Florida Atlantic University for his patience and invaluable advice as I completed this project. I especially appreciate Lady Bird Johnson's personal secretary, Shirley James for always being willing to spend time on the phone to provide me with valuable information. I must say that the archive staff at the Lyndon Baines Johnson Library in Austin is very helpful and was always willing to find any information in a timely and efficient manner. I particularly wish to think Claudia Anderson of the Johnson Library for her help in locating oral histories, articles and speeches. Ms. Anderson and her support staff are extremely excellent.

I wish to thank Jennifer Quann of the John F. Kennedy Library Foundation for her assistance in my request to quote portions of Jacqueline Kennedy Onassis'

December 1963 letter to Mrs. Johnson. Per the wishes of Mrs. Onassis' estate, I have kept the contents of that letter out of this work.

I want to extend my heartfelt appreciation to Mrs. Johnson's White House Social Secretary Bess Abell for taking the time for a personal interview. Also, I wish to thank former United Press International White House correspondent Helen Thomas for agreeing to a personal interview also. Someone else who was helpful was Mrs. Johnson's White House Press Secretary, Elizabeth Carpenter who spent a few minutes on the phone to verify some information, and for that I am extremely grateful.

If I forget someone, you know that I appreciate your support and inspiration as I completed this book.

David Murphy
Frankfort, Kentucky
December 2004

Chapter 1

THE BRICK HOUSE

CHILDHOOD

Lady Bird is certainly her mother's child. Minnie Taylor was well known around Karnack as an avid reader and friend of the environment. Her friends remember her returning from seeing TJ Taylor with a bunch of wildflowers in her hand. Lady Bird was only five when her mother passed away and she said years later, "I wish I knew more about her." She did say, "My memory of her is being tall and moving around very fast and dressing a lot in white and yes, there is something on her head." Indeed, everyone in town noticed Minnie was always wearing a large hat and a veil. Mrs. Taylor suffered migraines and used the veil to keep out sunlight, which was believed to bring on such headaches.

Lady Bird can even trace her social activism and political interest to her mother. She had a bird bath built in the front yard of the Brick House so she could feed and watch the birds throughout the year. Hunters were threatening the local quail population in 1910, so Minnie started a Save the Quail Society. Hunting was banned on thousands of acres of Taylor property but she allowed hunting at the end of the season to help control the quail population. [1]

Minnie Taylor was an early advocate for women to have the right to vote and was active in local campaigns. One of her granddaughters, Susan Taylor, said, "My grandmother loved politics and wanted nothing more than for women to be able to vote. Here Aunt Lady Bird came along and campaigned in every state of the union and wound up living in the White House. She fulfilled my grandmother's wildest dreams." Mrs. Taylor was no doubt smiling down on her daughter from heaven as she planted wildflowers across the nation and spoke out on the important issues of the day.

At the same time, her father was making a fortune from shrewd business deals. The sign on his store read, "Dealer in Everything." And that he was: he sold food, school supplies, thread, clothes, medicine, and farm tools. Most of the money was made by what was then known as advancing. He would loan (or advance) land, farm equipment, and seeds to tenant farmers in the spring, then make a profit in the following autumn when the cotton crop came in.

Taylor was also known for lending black families money, then taking their land as payment for the debt. One such family, the Haggertys, gave half of their one-hundred acre farm to Taylor to pay off some debts. However, Taylor took sixty acres and Haggerty said "When you deal to Boss Taylor, he takes a bit."

In 1914, Taylor bought the Haggerty family's original five thousand acre homestead. Records show that by 1918, he had made $43,387.50 from cotton and corn grown on seven hundred acres of the Haggerty land. The sell of hogs, horses, and left over cotton seeds also made Taylor a profit.[2]

Mr. Taylor was a well know ladies man, and he and Minnie had separated for some time, but reconciled by 1910. He purchased his wife the Brick House as part of the reconciliation and Minnie loved the large dining room with a stone fire place. After two miscarriages, Minnie became in pregnant in March 1912 at the age of thirty-eight. A healthy baby girl was born in an upstairs bedroom in the early morning of December 22. The baby was named Claudia Alta Taylor, after Minnie's brother, Claud.

TJ was excited and wrote and told Minnie's sister Effie in Billings, Alabama, "She really is very pretty, and Minnie is very proud of her. She had a remarkably easy time. We had, though, the best doctor in Marshall and a trained nurse. The nurse is still with us, though Minnie is up, and I believe and hope that she is going to be better than she ever was."[3]

There are two conflicting reports as to how Claudia received the nickname, "Lady Bird." Claudia always said herself that she got the name when her black nurse, Alice Tittle said she was as "purty as a lady bird," referring to a popular beetle of the Karnack region. But, James Cato Pattillo, an Alabama cousin, recalled that Claudia's father repeated a famous nursery rhyme when he heard of her birth, "Lady-bird, Lady-bird, fly away home, your house is on fire and your children will burn." Pattillo noted that refrain was often used "at times of outstanding events." At any rate, the nickname stuck and years later her brother, Antonio Taylor said, "the poor gal tried to shake it but it vain."

The birth had left Minnie weak and her health didn't approve as TJ had hoped. So, the two boys were sent to the Riordan School for Boys in New York. Minnie sent for information about possible boarding schools for Lady Bird when she was still just an infant.

Two events Lady Bird witnessed as a child influenced her thinking of society and made her more supportive of equality. When she was five, she remembered getting a new doll, teddy bear, firecrackers, oranges, and walnuts for Christmas. When she went over to see what her two friends, children of the black servants had got for Christmas, all they got were clothes. Her mother gave her no definite answer when Lady Bird questioned this, but this was an early lesson for the young girl on how the two races were treated differently.

She also recalled an incident that sparked her passionate support for civil rights. "I remember once when I was a little girl that a group of white mine cornered a black man in the middle of the night and accused of him of some crime." Needless to say, the man was petrified and ran off. As he ran, one of the white men shot him in the back. Lady Bird recalled thinking to herself, "This isn't right. Somebody ought to change this."[4]

Mother and daughter went door-to-door campaigning against a candidate for county commissioner that Minnie didn't like. Robert Hope, the candidate, had stayed home from World War I to work on his father's farm, for that, Minnie thought him to be a slacker. Indeed, Mr. Taylor was supporting Hope, so Minnie was being brave, for going against one's husband was a bold thing to do in those days. Therefore it can be said that Lady Bird inherited her mother's boldness and habit of speaking her mind, regardless of what others may think or say.

More mother and daughter campaign outings were not to be. Minnie was forty-four years old and became pregnant at that risky age in the fall of 1918. She fell down a flight of stairs at the Brick House and had to be rushed to a nearby hospital. So, at the tender age of five and a half, Lady Bird was brought to her mother's deathbed. Years later, she was able to recall the moment. "She looked over at me and said, 'My poor little girl, her face is dirty." So, her nurse, Alice Tittle, gave her mother a washcloth to wash Lady Bird's face with. She said her mother then fell back into bed and cried, "Nobody at home to care for you but the black nurse. Poor child."[5] Later on that day, September 14, 1918, Minnie Taylor passed away.

Mr. Taylor did not tell his sons of their mother's death for a nearly a year. She was laid to rest in a Confederate cemetery near Scottsville, Texas. Later on, her youngest son, Tony had an epitaph etched on her headstone, "Forgetful of self, she lived only for others." Lady Bird didn't attend the services, and her father was worried about who would take care of her now that her mother was gone. His work had to continue since the fall of the year was when tenants cashed in their crops to pay off their debts. For the first few months following Minnie's death, Taylor took his daughter to work with him and made her bed on the second floor of the store. She missed her mother and felt sorry for her father because of the burdens he now carried.

Year later, Lady Bird recalled how she pretended to see her mother flying across the sky in a chariot. She said, "Often, when there were clouds or sunset or something dramatic in the sky, I would somewhat expect that if I looked at in the right angle, I might indeed see her. But, I never did."[6] This explains why Lady Bird enjoyed the outdoors and nature as much as she did. Minnie had enjoyed the outdoors, and Lady Bird felt closest to her mother while communing with nature. We can imagine Lady Bird looking up at a bright blue sky and seeing her mother smiling down on her.

STARTING SCHOOL

Despite hard feelings he felt toward the Pattillos, Taylor put his daughter on a train to Alabama so her Aunt Effie could take care of her. He put a sign around her neck, "Deliver this child to John Will Pattillo." Lady Bird was excited to travel that far and was not afraid. Effie and Lady Bird returned to Karnack in time for Lady Bird to start school. She attended Fern School Number 14, where seven grades were taught in one room. There were fourteen students, all white. Lady Bird's favorite period of the school week was Friday afternoons when the class would line up and sing songs like "America the Beautiful."

The school closed when Lady Bird was in the seventh grade, so the teacher moved into the Brick House with her so Lady Bird could continue her education at home. She would take breaks from studying to go swimming or on picnics. Not being subjected to the racial tensions in the South, she played with black children of the Brick House workers, and even went to church with them on Sundays.

In 1925, Lady Bird and Effie moved to Jefferson so Lady Bird could begin high school. Her older brother, Tommy had opened a store in the town, which was thirteen miles from Karnack. Effie and Lady Bird stayed at the home of Bernice Emmett, who belonged to the Jamie Allen Wise Garden Club, which ran the little town of 2,600.

It was in Jefferson that Lady Bird found her first romance. She went to several dances with J. H. Benefield who said she was "one of the most determined persons I met in my life, one of the most ambitious and able."[7] Even as a teenager, people were seeing Lady Bird as a strong and determined woman who was going places. One of Lady Bird's earlier beaus made a prophetic statement when you consider how her life turned out. Thomas C. Soloman said that with Lady Bird "it would take a strong man to be the boss."[8]

By her high school years, the pattern was the Lady Bird and Effie would spend the summer in Alabama, and the school year in Karnack. Lady Bird moved back home in 1926 so she could attend high school in Marshall. Her father bought her a Chevrolet coupe so she could drive the fifteen miles to Marshall. The young Lady Bird continued to find solace in nature. She enjoyed solitary boat rides on Caddo Lake to enjoy the moss hanging down from the Cypress Trees. She created a ceremony to name the first daffodil that bloomed in the season the queen.

Lady Bird was a successful student studying law, Latin, geometry, physics, and communication. She made all A's and received A+'s in law and Latin. She dreaded public speaking so purposely allowed her grades to slip so that she would not have to speak as the valedictorian or salutatorian. Her best friend, Emma Boehringer was first place, and Lady Bird graduated third in her class at the age of 15. Marshall High School students had a tradition of predicting each other's 0future. Of Lady Bird, someone wrote that she would become, "a second Halliburton, poking her nose in unknown places in Asia."

ENDNOTES

[1] Jan Jarboe Russell, *Lady Bird: A Biography of Mrs. Johnson* (New York, Scribner, 1999) p. 44
[2] Russell, p. 49
[3] Russell, p. 51
[4] Russell, p. 52
[5] Russell, p. 53
[6] Russell, p. 55
[7] Russell, p. 66
[8] Russell, p. 60

Chapter 2

THE FIRST DATE

ENTERING THE GATES OF THE WORLD

Lady Bird wasted no time in furthering her education after high school. She immediately enrolled in summer school at the University of Alabama, taking two hours of journalism and four hours of history. However, she was lonely for her Texas friends. Her friend from high school, Helen Bird, was applying to the St. Mary's Episcopal School for Girls in Dallas and recommended Lady Bird do the same.

Her father and namesake uncle Claud Pattillo strongly objected, but Lady Bird helf firm and enrolled in St. Mary's in the fall of 1928. Lady Bird was fortunate enough to be able to room with Helen Bird since the school enforced strict curfews, and no girl was to leave campus without a chaperone. It was at St. Mary's that she became an Episcopalian, a faith tradition she has kept to this day. Her official confirmation took place in 1933 at St. David's Episcopal Church in Austin. Due to her Bible classes at St. Mary's Lady Bird said, "God didn't seem less real or awesome to me, just bigger and more complex."

She excelled in every subject at St. Mary's but Chemistry, in which she made a D. Other than that, she made straight A's. She graduated from St. Mary's in 1930 and decided to spend the last two years of college at the University of Texas in Austin. Emma Boehringer's older sister, Gene, was going there and Emma suggested it to Lady Bird.

Lady Bird went alone on a chartered flight to Austin to visit the university and a field of bluebonnets caught her eyes as the plane was landing. She instantly fell in love with Austin saying, "It was as though the gates of the world flung open for me. I felt in love with lives itself."[1]

She was greeted at the airport by Gene Boehringer who was working as secretary to C. V. Terrell, chairman of the Texas Railroad Commission. Terrell was in a powerful position as he regulated Texas' supply of gas and oil. Therefore Gene got to know powerful people in Austin such as the governor's secretary and a young man named Lyndon Baines Johnson who was a secretary to Congressman Dick Kleberg of Kingsville.

Gene showed Lady Bird around Austin and she fell in love with the city and persuaded her father to let her attend the University of Texas at Austin (UT). It took some persuasion of Mr. Taylor, but he finally told Gene, "All right, as long as you take care of her." Lady Bird was excited at the opportunity to live and study in the heart of political power in Texas. A college education was a way to avoid poverty, especially at the height of the Great Depression. Tuition in those days was twenty-five dollars a year and you had unlimited use of the library for seven dollars a year.

Lady Bird chose to board at 301 West Twenty-first Street at a house ran by a Mrs. Matthews, who rented her three second floor bedrooms to female college students. She shared a double bed with Cecille Harrison, a sophomore from San Antonio. Harris was thrilled that Lady Bird provided a brand new down comforter for the bed. She noticed that Lady Bird didn't focus much on fashion, though Taylor provided his daughter with a charge account at Neiman-Marcus. Lady Bird said she wanted people to like her just as she was, not for her clothes. She also developed a reputation of being a very serious student. One of her UT friends, Emily Crowe said of Lady Bird, "She was very conscientious about her studies, a lot more than Cecille and I."[2]

Ambitions were very restricted for women in those days, so Lady Bird is to be praised for pursuing an education at UT, instead of pursuing a social life. She spent the weekends with her friends, Emily, Cecille, and Gene driving her black Buick up and down the "Drag" in Austin. They would often stop at a drive-in and then drive around looking at wildflowers.

Lady Bird had several boyfriends while at UT saying, "I fell in love every April.[3] She attended a dance with Chilton O'Brien, president of the UT student body. She also dated Victor McRea, a law student and Jack Mayfield, who would become a prominent Houston surgeon. Gene Boehringer introduced Lady Bird to Dawson Duncan, who covered Texas politics for the *Dallas Morning News*. It was he who sparked her interest in journalism. Lady Bird graduated in May 1933 with a bachelor of arts in journalism and stayed an extra year to earn a second degree in journalism.

Gene was a supporter of Texas governor Ma Ferguson and Lady Bird got to know Ferguson's personal secretary, Gladys Little. With her boyfriend, Dawson

Duncan and Little, Lady Bird was aware of the all the important issues of the day, and she enjoyed being in the center of action. However, graduation forced Lady Bird to contemplate her future. She had wrote off about teaching positions in Alaska and Hawaii since she had earned a second-grade teaching certificate and also considered work as a secretary as a path to a business career.

Before getting on with her future, her father had agreed to fund a trip for Lady Bird as a graduation present. Lady Bird and Cecille Harrison decided to go to Washington, D.C. and New York City. Gene was excited that Lady Bird was going to Washington since she wanted Lady Bird to meet Lyndon Johnson. Gene gave her Lyndon's number and wrote and told him that Lady Bird was coming.

Cecille and Lady Bird took a boat to New York and they went shopping when the boat stopped in Miami Once in New York, they stayed at the Taft Hotel and was able to see some Broadway shows. Then, the two friends took a bus down to Washington and checked into the Wardman-Park Hotel. Lady Bird's boyfriend, Victor McRea was now a lawyer at the Postmaster General's office and he showed Lady Bird and Cecille around Washington. The girls were able to see the Lincoln, Jefferson, and Washington monuments, the Supreme Court, the Capitol, and the White House. She and McRea were having such a good time that she decided not to call Lyndon Johnson. It never occurred to Lady Bird as she went around Washington that she would spend the next thirty-five years of her life there.

A CHANCE MEETING

Lady Bird was in Austin two weeks after her trip and stopped in to see Gene at the Texas Railway Commission. Gene finally got the moment she had been waiting for. Lyndon Johnson was in the office to meet Gene's roommate, Dorothy for a date. He asked all of the three girls out for a drink. Lady Bird said of the young man that she had just met, "He was very, very good looking. Lots of hair, quite black and wavy, and the most outspoken, straightforward, determined young man I'd ever met. I knew I had met someone remarkable, but I didn't quite know who."[4] She was very mesmerized by him as she watched and listened to the future president interact with all three girls at once, not making one of them feel left out. As he left, he asked Lady Bird out for breakfast the following morning, "Meet me in the dining room of the Driskill Hotel." Without even thinking, Lady Bird said, "Okay."

So on the morning of August 31, 1934, Lady Bird went to downtown Austin. However, she was still debating whether or not to keep the date with Lyndon. She was meeting the architect Hugo Cuney to discuss the renovation of the Brick House. But, she wanted to break free of Karnack and not be tied down to a home setting like her mother and Aunt Effie. So it surely crossed her mind that Lyndon could be her ticket out of Karnack. Years later Lady Bird recalled, "He came on very strong and my first instinct was to withdraw."[5]

Withdrawing was her final decision, but that was made difficult by the fact that the architects office was next door to the Driskill dining room. Lyndon was determined not to let her go and noticed her attempting to avoid the dining room. He got out of his seat and waved both arms and put himself in Lady Bird's path. She had no choice but to set down, and he was very relieved. Lyndon recalled in a 1964 interview that if he hadn't stopped her, he thought that Lady Bird would never have kept the date.

Sitting there drinking a coffee, she listened to Lyndon and the more he talked, the more she grew to like him. He asked her about her family and future ambitions. He told her every detail of his life from his work for the congressman to how he was raised. Lady Bird, longing to break free and move on to bigger and better things was enamored by Lyndon and his being on the front lines as FDR battled to get the New Deal through Congress. She listened with envy and admiration as he told her about attending Roosevelt's first inaugural.

Next Lyndon took Lady Bird riding in one of Congressman Kleberg's convertibles that had leather seats. While driving around, he told Lady Bird about his future plans. "He talked a great deal about his job, about wanting to be best at whatever he did, about all the things he wanted to do. At the end of the day, he leaned over to Lady Bird and asked her to marry him. At first she thought he was joking. But, he said, "Listent, you are seeing the best of me." Which was indeed true, she was seeing the side of Lyndon Johnson that had bold dreams for his future of helping Americans out of poverty by one day holding office himself. As opposed to the domineering and cunning Lyndon that would do anything to obtain power and could be rude, even to those he loved. Also, it has been alleged that Johnson was not faithful to Lady Bird. For reasons known only to her, Lady Bird remained a faithful wife and trusted political partner. Who knows if the charges of adultery are true? As UPI White House correspondent Helen Thomas said thirty years after his passing, "Dead men can't defend themselves."

He was so determined to get Lady Bird to marry him that he insisted she meet his mother, Rebekah. The very next day after their first date, Lyndon drove Lady Bird to San Marcos to visit his family, which was not as well off as the Taylors. They lived in a rented house, and it was obvious to Lady Bird that the family had second-hand furniture. She said of Rebekah, "My first impression of her was that she was an elegant woman in less then elegant circumstances." His father, Sam was bed fast due to heart problems.

Rebekah was cold toward Lady Bird, for she feared that she would take Lyndon away from her. They would enjoy a distant relationship for the rest of Rebekah's life. The future First Lady said of her, "I saw her as an absolutely lovely woman, who had given too much to her husband and family."[6] That is bitterly ironic as that would be said of Lady Bird herself years later. She gave up dreams of being a journalist, perhaps a drama critic, to serve her husband and help him in his career.

Lyndon Johnson vowed to have a better life for himself than his parents had. To show Lady Bird that kind of person he hoped to become and the type of people he associated with, he drove her to Corpus Christi. There, he took her on a tour of King Ranch, Congressman Kleberg's sprawling Texas estate. Upon meeting Lady Bird, Kleberg's mother Alice told Lyndon. "Listen. Don't lose that girl. She's the best thing that could happen to you." Lady Bird saw Alice Kleberg as a queen and was thus somewhat ill at ease around her. However, Mrs. Kleberg was not shy and told Lady Bird as she left, "You should marry him."

But, Lady Bird was not ready to make such a commitment to Lyndon. She did invite him to Karnack to meet her father, and he accepted. Driving from Corpus Christi, Lyndon told her that he thought of Kleberg's district as his own and told Lady Bird to start learning the names of the counties and the problems and issues of the district. This gave her a preview of what her life as a Congressional spouse would be like.

Lyndon stopped at the Brick House on his way to Washington. He spent the night there along with Malcolm Baldwell, an aide to Congressman Maury Maverick. Mr. Taylor listened with deep interest as Lyndon told stories about Washington over dinner. After the meal, when it was just Lady Bird and Mrs. Taylor, he told her, "You've been bring home a lot of boys. This one looks like a real man."

Before he left, Lyndon gave Lady Bird a book, *Nazism: An Assault on Civilization*, a collection of essays by German journalist about the rising threat posed by the rise of the Nazi Party. He inscribed the book, "To Bird, in the hope within these pages, she may realize some little entertainment and find reiterated here some of the principles in which she believes and which she has been taught to revere and respect. LBJ." She in return gave him a copy of Voltaire's *Candide*, but she doubted he ever read it.

Lady Bird and Lyndon kept up their romance by letters and long-distance phone calls while he was away in Washington. His letters told all about his life in Washington and his plans for the future. She wanted to wait at least a year before getting married but Lyndon wrote, "Every interesting place I see, I make a mental reservation and tell myself that I should take you there when you are mine. I want to go through the museum, the Congressional library, the Smithsonian, the Civil War battlefields, and all of those interesting places. Why must we wait twelve long months to begin to do the things we want to do forever and ever?"[7] Lady Bird ended her October 1, 1934 letter, "In all sincerity, Lyndon, I believe I miss you more and more all the time. Goodnight my dearest dear, I love you, Bird."

She begins to grow lonely in Karnack, and Lyndon's pleas for marriage begin to look more attractive to her as the autumn of 1934 approached. Johnson wrote on October 21 and gave here a sampling of what life in politics would be like, "This morning, I'm, ambitious, proud, energetic, and very madly in love with you. I want to see people. I want to walk through the throngs, want to do things with a drive. If I had a box, I would almost make a speech this minute. Plans, ideas, hopes, I'm bubbling over with them." He had enrolled at Georgetown University Law School in September and ended the letter, "How much a young man in law school can hope? Tell me you love me if you want to, and if you don't, I'll believe you do anyway and keep on loving you every minute."[8]

After consulting with her Aunt Effie and a relative, Ellen Cooper Taylor, Lady Bird decided to marry Lyndon. That fall of 1934, Lyndon was weighing all his options on how to better himself and become wealthy. Lady Bird wrote to him on October 22, "Lyndon, please tell me as soon as you can what the deal is. Oh, I know I haven't any business—not any propelling interest—but I would hate for you to go into politics. Don't let me get things any more muddled for you than they are, dearest. I still love you, Lyndon, I want to say it over and over, goodnight, not goodbye, Bird."

Chiding her for her indecisive tone, Lyndon replied, "You see something you might want. You tear it pieces in an effort to determine if you should want it. Then you wonder why you want it, and conclude that maybe the desire isn't an 'everlasting' one and that the 'sane' thing to do is to waste a year or so, and then if you still want it, to decide at that time whether or not you should make an effort to get it."

Lyndon's mind was made up. Lady Bird returned to the Brick House for Alabama on November 16 to find Lyndon on the front porch waiting for her. Johnson quit law school and asked Lady Bird to marry him telling her, "We either do it now, or we never will." So, on November 17, 1934, Lady Bird Taylor and Lyndon Baines Johnson were married and headed for a honeymoon to Monterrey, Mexico the next day. She and Lyndon got to see San Louis Potosi and Mexico City and Mrs. Johnson knew that her life would never quite be the same again.

ENDNOTES

[1] Russell, p.72
[2] Russell, p. 77
[3] Russell, p. 81
[4] Russell, p. 90
[5] Russell, p. 92
[6] Russell, p. 102
[7] Russell, p. 107
[8] Rusell, p. 109

Chapter 3

THE CONGRESSWOMAN FROM TEXAS

MRS. JOHNSON GOES TO WASHINGTON

Once back in Washington, Lady Bird found that Johnson worked around the clock and she was to help him by running the "home" office. She did convince him to move out of his tiny apartment and move into a one-bedroom furnished apartment at 1910 Kalorama Road of which Lady Bird was housekeeper. She also saw to it that all the bills were promptly paid, which she enjoyed after watching her father manage money all those years.

Lady Bird decided, with the urging of Terrell Maverick, wife of Congressman Maverick, to become fully involved in Johnson's political life and get to know his network of friends. She begun by having the Congressman and Mrs. Maverick over to the Johnson's place for dinner. Lady Bird spent as much time in the living room as possible so she could listen to her husband and Maverick discussed the goings on of Capitol Hill. Another couple that frequented the Johnson's apartment was the Clifford Durrs. He was in town working as one of the three heads of the FCC under FDR and would later become famous when he represented Rosa Parks after her famous arrest that launched the civil rights movement. Virginia Durr recalled how Lyndon would talk of ending poverty and say of Lady Bird, "She just looked at him with worshipping eyes and let him hold the floor, and he did hold the floor and he held it very well."

Congressman Kleberg suggested that Lyndon find another job, and President Roosevelt made a way for Lyndon and millions of other young people unemployed just like him with the creation of the National Youth Administration (NYA) in June 1935. Lyndon asked Congressman Maverick to help him get appointed by FDR as the Texas director of the NYA. By August, he and Lady

Bird moved into a two story home in Austin since Lyndon had become the youngest NYA director in the country. The annual salary was $7,500, about twice as much as he was making in Washington.

Gladys Montgomery, who along with her husband Bob, the Johnsons were renting their house from, made a suggestion of a possible project for the Texas NYA. She recommended roadside parks be constructed along Texas highways to provide drivers a safe place to pull over in an emergency or for some rest. Fifteen thousand young Texans were put to work building the parks as well as planting grass, brick laying, and mural painting. The landscaping of the roadside sparks made Lady Bird aware of how public resources could be used to improve the beauty of the nation.

Being back in Texas helped Lyndon's political career a great deal. He was traveling around the state, getting recognition as the head of the NYA and forging friendships that would help him in political campaigns. His first opportunity came in February 1937 when Congressman James Buchanan died suddenly of a heart attack. Johnson decided to seek the seat representing the Tenth Congressional District of Texas. Lady Bird jumped right into the effort and sought the advice of former state senator Alvin Wirtz. She said, "He told me that Lyndon was a long shot because he was the least known of the any of the people who were going to run, but he thought Lyndon had a chance."[1] When Wirtz told her that the campaign would cost $10,000, she convinced her father to transfer $10,000 of her inheritance to the Johnson's bank account.

Lady Bird worked hard, mostly behind the scenes, in the forty-two day campaign. For his part, Lyndon visited every county in the district and shook as many hands as possible. The odds didn't look good for Lyndon when he had to have an emergency appendectomy just two days before the election. Lady Bird was by his side in the hospital, but worked the phones on Election Day to get out the vote for her husband. Johnson won the race, proving Lady Bird's ability as a political wife. He was sworn in on May 13, 1937 while Lady Bird rested from the campaign in Karnack. It was around this time that Lyndon brought on John Connally as one of his key aides. The friendship between the Johnsons and John and Nellie Connally would last a lifetime, thought John Connally became more conservative than Lyndon as the years went on.

On April 9, 1941, Senator Morris Sheppard passed away so Lyndon decided to run for the vacant seat in a special election that was held on June 28. Johnson had no hard time raising campaign funds since the George and Herman Brown brothers who owned a Houston construction company contributed $300,000 and another $200,000 was raised from other business men such as *Austin-American Statesman* publisher Charles Marsh.

In the campaign, Johnson faced an uphill battle against the sitting governor, Willie Lee "Pappy" O'Daniel who was the owner of the Hillbilly Flour Company and lead a western band whose weekly radio show was broadcast all over the state. Johnson's own polls showed him getting a distant 9% of the vote compared to O'Daniel's 33%.

Connally helped with the campaign by forming a network made up primarily of Johnson's college friends. Lady Bird made home movies of campaign events and calmed her husband's nerves when the polls didn't turn out well. Johnson checked himself into a clinic for depression in the middle of the campaign. It was Lady Bird who urged him to get out and back on the campaign trail. She was backed up in her efforts by a poll showing her husband at 17.9%. She would have that calming effect on him for the rest of their marriage, raising his spirits when events weren't going his way.

When the ballots were counted, Johnson was ahead by 5,150 votes, but O'Daniel asked for a recount. Five days later, O'Daniel was declared the winner by a margin of 1,311 votes. Johnson was devastated and wanted to resign his House seat, but Lady Bird told him to just be patient for there would be other Senate campaigns.

Lady Bird was settled well in the role of Congressional wife. She took constituents around to see the sights of Washington and kept up to date with the people of the district. She had calling cards made to call on the wives of Cabinet members, Senate wives, other House wives, Supreme Court wives, and the wives of the Diplomatic Corp. Of course, she always attended the White House when invited. This simple life as a Washington wife was about to hit by a huge shockwave, as well as the lives of all Americans.

"CONGRESSWOMAN" AND BUSINESSWOMAN JOHNSON

The Japanese attacked Pearl Harbor on December 7, 1941 and Lyndon immediately joined the Navy. President Roosevelt assigned him and John Connally to Secretary of State James Forrestal. They went away to the Pacific theater so Nellie Connally and Lady Bird moved into a one-bedroom apartment in Buckingham, Virginia that rented for sixty dollars a month. Lyndon had Lady Bird take over the management of his Congressional office, and Nellie assisted Lady Bird in that effort. Mrs. Johnson handled any constituent problems, lead tours, and signed letters sent to Lyndon. In effect, she was the "Congresswoman" in her husband's absence.

Lyndon returned on July 10, 1942, but his time away convinced Lady Bird that she could make a living on her own. With that in mind, she pursued the purchase of KTBC, a small Austin radio station. With money from the inheritance left by hermother, she wrote a $17,500 check on December 31, 1942. The FCC approved the sale on February 16, 1943, and Lady Bird went into the office to find ways for the station to start turning a profit. She carefully went over the books and started immediately to find ways to save money. Later on, in 1943, the FCC granted Mrs. Johnson's request to increase the power of the station so it could broadcast twenty-four hours a day. She oversaw the transfer of KTBC into a television station and founded the Texas Broadcasting System, and by the time she was First Lady, *Life* estimated her worth to be $9 million. Lady Bird was the first First Lady to accumulate and maintain wealth on her own.

Also in 1942, Lady Bird convinced her husband to purchase a home in Washington; she had grown tired of moving so much. So they moved into a two-story house at 4912 Thirtieth Place, across the street from J. Edgar Hoover. Now, she just wanted to have children to bring in the new house. After several miscarriages, she became pregnant in the late summer of 1943. She managed the station from home in Washington, and on March 19, 1944, Lynda Bird Johnson was born. She started back up her commute between Washington and Austin. However, she became pregnant again in late 1946, and Lucy Baines Johnson was born on July 2, 1947. So, the entire Johnson family had the now famous "LBJ" initials.

ENDNOTES

---

[1] Russell, p. 130

Chapter 4

THE GREAT ADVENTURE

LANDSLIDE LYNDON

By the time the girls made it to elementary school, they had a caretaker, Willie Day Taylor, who spent the half the year in Austin with them. Taylor and the girls spent the other half of the year in Washington. Lady Bird had hire a fulltime black cook, Zephyr Wright in 1942, who went all the way to the White House with the Johnsons. Lucy and Lynda had to early on make peace with the fact that their mother put their father first. However, she taught her daughters to revere their father for his chosen career and to take advantage of his position to observe history being made.

Johnson got his opportunity to run again for a Senate seat when he decided to run against incumbent Senator Coke Stevenson in 1948. Lady Bird stood by his side at the May 22 night rally where he officially announced his candidacy, though he was in immense pain due to a kidney stone. He made it through the rally with pain medication from doctors and checked into a Dallas hospital the following morning.

Lyndon got angry when Connally announced his illness to the press, and threatened to withdraw from the race. Warren Woodward, a young campaign aide, was at a lost as to what to do and called Lady Bird in desperation. She arrived at the hospital and talked to her husband alone and persuaded him to stay in the campaign just as she had managed to do when he made the same threats in 1941. The Johnsons flew to the Mayo Clinic on May 27 where the kidney stone was removed by inserting an instrument through Lyndon's urethra, making an incision unnecessary.

Lady Bird got deeply involved with the 1948 campaign, since she felt guilty for not doing more in Lyndon's 1941 Senate campaign. She made speeches and joined in on strategy sessions with aides such as Connally and Alvin Wirtz. Texas was such a vast, sprawling state that Lyndon sought an innovative way for his campaign to reach the entire state. He chose to use a helicopter to make his rounds throughout the state, and Lady Bird accompanied him and made home movies of the campaign events. The film shows Johnson hanging out the door of the helicopter saying into a microphone, "Hello, down there. There is Lyndon Johnson, your candidate for the United States Senate."[1]

The day before ballots were cast, Lady Bird joined Rebekah Johnson and Lyndon's three sisters at the Austin campaign headquarters to make calls to get out the vote. They simply worked their way through the Austin phone book. The election was a cliffhanger for when the votes were counted, Stevenson was ahead by 113 votes. However, the ballots from infamous Box Number 13 came in from South Texas, and that put Lyndon ahead by eighty-seven votes. Stevenson tried challenging the election in the courts, but Lyndon Johnson was sworn in to the Senate in January 1949 at the age of forty. Due to the close he election, he was known as "Landslide Lyndon."

Now, that he was in the Senate, Johnson wanted the kind of estate suitable for hosting fellow politicians and friends, similar to Congressman Kleberg's King Ranch. The opportunity presented itself in 1951 when his Aunt Frank offered the deed to her 243 acre ranch for around $20,000. The ranch was located near Stonewall and its two-story house overlooked the Pedernales River. By this time, KTBC was turning a profit as the earnings of 1951 were $57,983 after taxes. With their financial situation such that they could afford it, Lyndon persuaded Lady Bird to let him purchase the ranch. She stayed there while in Austin to oversee the transformation of the property into the now famous LBJ Ranch.

Lady Bird's business continued to prosper as the 1950s went along. She decided to apply for a television license and opted for the one very high frequency (VHF) station that the FCC was allotting to Austin, and the FCC granted her request on July 11, 1952. Lyndon used his connections to obtain contracts from KTBC from all the major networks, CBS, ABC, and NBC. Therefore, the station had a monopoly on the airwaves of Austin and was able to charge $575 an hour for advertising as compared to the $325 an hour charged by the Minneapolis-St. Paul station. By 1959, KTBC was worth $2,569,503.

Lady Bird continued to enjoy her role as a Congressional wife, and went to Lyndon's office several times a week and brought the stuff Texas shaped cookies and had the Senate Dining Room served Texas shaped hamburgers to Lyndon's guests. She enjoyed going to the Senate gallery and observing debate. Speaker of the House Sam Rayburn was a frequent guest at the Johnson's home, and she enjoyed listening to he and Lyndon discuss the politics of passing legislation. One evening at dinner, Lady Bird served Rayburn Turkey hash and she a got a swift scolding from Lyndon, "Can't you serve the speaker of the house anything better than turkey hash?" Rayburn stood up for Lady Bird telling Lyndon that he wished he had more turkey hash in Washington. Once Rayburn left, Lady Bird told Lyndon not to ever raise questions about her food in front of guest again. He just nodded vigorously. Lady Bird was never afraid to speak her mind to Lyndon and let him know when his behavior or language offended her. In any such circumstance she would often say, "Lyndon!" in a tart, strict voice.

Lyndon had a quick rise to power in the Senate, being elected Majority Leader in January of 1955. He spent his tenure bridging the divide between conservative Democrats like Richard Russell of Georgia and liberals like Stuart Symington of Missouri. However, his health slowed him down in his first few months as Majority Leader. He once again entered the Mayo Clinic for a kidney stone operation on January 18. Lady Bird went with him to the ranch to assist him in his recovery. Bad health continued the rest of that spring, as he didn't watch his diet, and ate whatever he wanted to, and smoked heavily.

Upon arriving at George Brown's Middlesburg, Virginia estate on July 2, he suffered a heart attack. A doctor was called in and Johnson had to be transported to Bethesda Naval Hospital in a hearse since no ambulances were available. Lady Bird, Walter Jenkins, and George Reedy were waiting at the hospital when Johnson arrived. Lyndon told his wife, "Stay with me, Bird. I'd rather fight with you by my side." He was placed into a oxygen tent and went into a shock, and the next forty-eight hours were critical. Having suffered a coronary occlusion, he had a fifty-fifty chance of survival.

Lady Bird moved into a room across from Lyndon's during his six week stay at the hospital and managed his Senate office for him. All important mail was sent to the hospital for her to sign. Lyndon later told Lady Bird's press secretary, Liz Carpenter, "During those long nights in the hospital, the first sound I heard every time I woke up was Lady Bird's foot hitting the floor, and running to my side."[2] He took medication for depression, a common affliction of heart attack survivors. Zephyr Wright made him low-fat meals at home and had them delivered to him so he didn't have to endure hospital food.

His recuperation period at the ranch was very difficult on him, Lady Bird, and the staff. It was difficult to make him follow doctor's orders, and he was always threatening to smoke a cigarette. He complained about the low-fat meals provided by Wright, but ate them anyway. Lyndon exercised by walking the mile to his cousins Oriole's house and swimming in the pool at the ranch. The efforts of Lady Bird and Wright paid off for Lyndon went from 225 pounds to 177 pounds.

Johnson returned to the Senate on January 3, 1956 and after Eisenhower's re-election, he found himself to be the nation's leading Democrat. Therefore, he sat his sights on the 1960 Democratic Presidential nomination. He did begin talk of not running again in 1962, but Lady Bird had heard Lyndon's threats to quit so much, that she simply ignored such talk. Lyndon was dealt a blow in 1958 when his mother died of cancer and his depression returned and he begin to drink more heavily. He once again resumed talk of retiring, and Lady Bird believed that he wouldn't seek the presidential nomination, especially in the condition he was in.

But, she had misread her husband for once, for the 1960 Democratic presidential nomination turned into a contest between Lyndon and fellow Senator, John F. Kennedy. Johnson and his staff arrived in Los Angeles for the Democratic convention on July 8, with the actual vote from the delegates to come on July 13. Lady Bird, Lynda, and Luci worked the floor on the night the delegates voted while Lyndon watched it from his hotel room. Kennedy received 806 votes to Johnson's 409. Lyndon told the press, "I lost fair and square," and seem to be relieved and upbeat. However, Lady Bird was not in such a good mood. She just stared at the television and cried, and Luci dressed in black saying, "My father has lost and I am in mourning and I want the whole world to know it."[3]

Mrs. Johnson was awakened the next morning at 7:30 by a secretary; Senator Kennedy was on the line for Lyndon. She walked quietly over to her husband's bed and asked him if he wanted to talk to Kennedy, he wasting no time in saying "Yes." Kennedy insisted on coming upstairs to meet with Senator Johnson, and Johnson told him to come on up. So, around 11 am, Kennedy arrived and talked to Johnson about the need for a strong running mate. Kennedy never offered the job to Johnson, and Johnson suggested Senator Hubert Humphrey or Senator Stuart Symington.

Over the course of the day, John Connally and Rayburn met with Bobby Kennedy, who told them that liberals would be upset if Johnson joined the ticket. Phil Graham, publisher of the *Washington Post*, was also a mediator between Kennedy and Johnson. Lady Bird was present when Rayburn told Graham and Lyndon that Bobby Kennedy wanted to meet with Lyndon. Lady Bird spoke up and said that she thought that her husband should deal with Senator Kennedy directly. Her husband, Rayburn and Graham and all agreed and Graham called Kennedy with the news that Johnson would only accept the vice presidency if Kennedy himself offered it to Johnson. Kennedy told Graham to call him back in a few minutes.

When Graham called Kennedy back at 2:45 in the afternoon, Kennedy told him that Johnson was indeed his choice for a running mate.

Johnson and his staff were not elated to being second to John F. Kennedy and blamed liberals and the Kennedy family's money for beating Johnson for the nomination. Years later Johnson recalled to historian Doris Kearns Goodwin of Kennedy, "He never said a word of importance in the Senate and he never did a thing. But somehow...he managed to create the image of himself as a shining intellectual, a youthful leader who would change the face of the country."[4]

THE GREAT ADVENTURE

Shortly after the convention, Lady Bird went to back to the ranch to contemplate her role in the campaign and decide the ways in which she can make a difference. Senator Kennedy put in a call to the ranch and explained to Lyndon that Mrs. Kennedy was pregnant and wanted to limit her campaigning due to fears of experiencing another miscarriage. "Would Lady Bird carry the load on the women's end of the campaign?" he asked. Lady Bird was listening on the other phone, and said, "Certainly."

It was around this time that Lady Bird called reporter Liz Carpenter and asked her to help with the campaign, "Lyndon asked me to call you, Liz, and see if you could take off from your newspapers until after the election. We'd like you to share the great adventure of our lives." She asked for three days to think it over, and her fear of flying made he think twice about accepting Johnson's offer. Her fourteen year old son told her, "There has never been a bird that crash-landed. And you'll be flying with Lady Bird." That helped to convince her to take the job and she went on to become Lady Bird's press secretary and office manager in the White House.[5]

The Kennedys had made great use of tea parties for women in their campaigns in Massachusetts and they wished to do the same during the 1960 campaign. Carpenter assisted Lady Bird in planning Texas tea parties to benefit the Kennedy-Johnson ticket. Lady Bird and Carpenter went through the list of names of political friends that the Johnsons had collected over the years. Mrs. Johnson called the women and her husband called the men to get people out to the teas.

Six teas were planned in Texas in Houston, Dallas, Wichita Falls, Odessa-Midland, El Paso, and the LBJ Ranch. Kennedy's sister, Eunice Shriver, and Ethel Kennedy, Bobby's wife, joined Lady Bird for the teas. Carpenter tried to get Eunice and Ethel to wear cowboy hats at a photo opportunity before they boarded the plane in Washington, but they wouldn't. "I kept thinking, if we had been up in Boston we would have been glad to put on a derby or a homburg. But they practically sat on those Texas hats."[6] That was the beginning of cultural differences between the Kennedys, who thought the Johnsons to be hicks. It was alleged during the campaign that Jackie Kennedy called the Johnsons "Senator Cornpone and Mrs. Pork Chop." Carpenter hoped that the Kennedy women would at least put on a good old act of being pro-Texans during the teas.

Senator Kennedy went to Houston to stress his independence from the Vatican by giving a speech to the Greater Houston Ministerial Association. That was the same time Lady Bird was hosting the Houston tea party with Ethel and Eunice. Around 5,025 women showed up to shake their hands, and the Kennedy women were growing restless. Carpenter reported this to Lady Bird who said, "But this is my state. I don't want to disappoint these women who have waited to see us." Lady Bird by then understands how personal politics is, and realized that a hand shake could be worth a vote.

On September 13, Lady Bird was debriefing Lyndon on the Houston tea party when a call came to their room from a doctor in Marshall. Lady Bird's father, T.J., now eighty-six, was in the hospital for blood poising of the leg and it would have to be amputated. She rushed back immediately to be at her father's side the next morning. As she met Kennedy and sat through his speech to the ministers, who expressions or manners gave no clue as to what had just happened with her father.

T. J. Taylor passed away on October 22, and Johnson raised some controversy by distributing campaign literature at the door before the funeral. Taylor left Lady Bird a brick office building in Missouri and a sizable portion of his $1 million estate when to his last wife, Ruth. Lady Bird was devastated that Ruth had inherited the Brick House. Mrs. Johnson tried up until the 1990s to convince Ruth to hand over the Brick House to her. Lady Bird even offered to support her, so long as she got the house. Ruth never budged, and Lady Bird could only see her childhood home from the roadside.

Lady Bird got back into the campaign and Jackie Kennedy sent her a donkey pin with sapphire eyes and diamond chip ears for Lady Bird to wear while campaigning. "The adorable golden donkey, who seems to be traveling at a fast clip, is so much appreciated and I will be wearing it with great pride," Lady Bird wrote Mrs. Kennedy in appreciation of the gift. She also sent Lady Bird a sympathy note right after her father's death, "What can one say to a friend who has lost a father in the midst of a presidential campaign?"

A pivotal moment of the campaign came on November 4 when Lyndon and Lady Bird were in Dallas. A crowd of four hundred white prominent Dallas women gathered at an intersection to block the Johnsons from walking across the street to a campaign event. The protest of Lyndon's liberalism was led by the only Republican Congressman from Texas, Bruce Alger. Signs read "LBJ Sold Out to Yankee Socialists" and "Lets Ground Lady Bird." One woman even spit in Lady Bird's face, and Lyndon put his hand over his wife's mouth to keep her quiet. This was all being broadcast on TV, and he knew the angry protest played against the Republicans. Lyndon kept his arm around Lady Bird as they made their way to the ballroom where he was to speak.

When Johnson got to the podium, he said, "If the time has come that I can't walk with my lady through the corridors of the hotels of Dallas, then I want to know about it." Joseph P. Kennedy, Junior had been killed on a secret mission during World War II and Lyndon evoked the memory when talking about religion, "They didn't ask Joe Kennedy, Junior what church he belonged to when he went on that mission." Lady Bird was tired from the whole ordeal and told Carpenter that she felt like "cooked spaghetti." Mrs. Johnson did recall, "I'll always remember that Stanley Marcus walked by his best charge customers to be a Democrat in Dallas publicly and that was not the popular thing to do."[7]

LADY BIRD CARRIED TEXAS

The Johnsons spent, November 8, election night, at the Driskill Hotel where there first date at been nearly thirty years ago. Kennedy was declared the winner at seven the next morning by a margin of 112,881 votes and he carried Texas by 46,330 votes as well as six other Southern states. Thinking of the teas and the angry protestors, "Well, Lady Bird carried Texas for the president."

Now that Lyndon was going to be vice-president, the Johnsons were in need of a bigger Washington home. They rented a four-bedroom apartment at the Sheraton Park Hotel right after election. Six month later, in April 1961, they moved into The Elms, a large French-style home located on a hill in the Spring Valley area of Washington.

Lady Bird hosted Senate wives at The Elms to lunches where she asked each woman to stand up and tell about her home state. Mrs. Johnson was called upon by the White House to fill in for Mrs. Kennedy at events such as meeting Girl Scout troops or a photo opportunity with the muscular dystrophy child. Indeed, in 1961 Lady Bird stood in for Jackie at over fifty official functions.

Lyndon was miserable in his new role, but he always performed any task that Kennedy assigned to him such as attending funerals of foreign dignitaries or attend meetings of NATO. Lyndon and Lady Bird were always invited to official

White House events, and if their names weren't on a list, President Kennedy would write them in.

One of Johnson's most famous foreign trips was to Senegal in 1961. Johnson was not above exploring the streets and marketplaces of Dakar to meet the people and let them know they had a friend in the United States. Lyndon even got out of his limo at Kayar, a small fishing village. He mingled among the villagers and even shook hands with a leper. Vice President Johnson said, "If they think they are going to meet me at an airport and put me past hundreds of people who want to shake hands with the United States of America embodied in me, well, they've got another thing coming."[8] The routine of Lyndon waiting around to be called upon by President Kennedy soon came to an abrupt and shocking end.

ENDNOTES

[1] Russell, p. 158
[2] Russell, p. 176
[3] Russell, p. 180
[4] Robert Dallek, *Flawed Giant: Lyndon Johnson and His Times: 1961-1973* (New York, Oxford, 1998)
[5] Liz Carpenter, *Ruffles and Flourishes* (Garden City, New York, Doubleday & Company, Inc.)
[6] Russell, p. 194
[7] Russell, p. 208
[8] Carpenter, 94

Childhood portrait of Lady Bird taken around 1915. (LBJ Library Photo from Taylor family collection, photographer unknown)

The Brick House in which Lady Bird was born and raised. (LBJ Library Photo from Taylor family collection, photographer unknown)

Chapter 5

TEXAS TRAGEDY

DALLAS

"It all began so beautifully. After a drizzle in the morning, the sun came out bright and clear. We were driving into Dallas." So begin Lady Bird's diary entry for Friday, November 22, 1963. Clear skies caused President Kennedy to delight in the fact that he did not need the bubble top on his car for the parade through Dallas. Being a seasoned political wife, Lady Bird was probably not surprised that the President wanted as many people as possible to see him. Reports were coming in that the Dallas streets were packed with well-wishers for the presidential motorcade. Proud of her native Texas, Lady Bird was relieved that the Kennedys appeared to be welcomed with open arms.

Worries abounded about that the kind of welcome President Kennedy would receive because U.N. Ambassador Adali Stevenson had been spat upon by protestors in Dallas a few weeks before the Kennedy visit. Lady Bird was likely recalling the time Lyndon and she were jostled and heckled by an angry crowd in Dallas during the 1960 campaign. No doubt that her fears were relieved by the happy, cheering crowds she saw as the motorcade made its way through downtown Dallas.

It is going to be a lovely weekend, Lady Bird thought to herself while riding in the parade. Texas had proven to be a natural kickoff for the 1964 campaign. After joining the Kennedys at several campaign stops, the Johnsons were to host the First Couple at the LBJ Ranch. Mrs. Johnson was hoping to herself that her Social Secretary Bess Abell would bring the Kennedys through the front door instead of through the kitchen, which was crammed full with twenty pecan pies, eighteen loaves of homemade bread, and simmering pots of barbecue sauce. So,

Lady Bird didn't want the socially refined Jacqueline Kennedy to enter the ranch through the kitchen door. She would have plenty of time to see to that later on, now all Lady Bird could do was sit back and enjoy the ride to the Dallas Trade Mart.

We all know what happened that terrible day. The motorcade never reached the Trade Mart and President Kennedy never made it to the LBJ Ranch. Lady Bird writes, "Suddenly, there was a sharp, loud rapport. It sounded like a shot." She heard two more shots in "rapid succession." It just had to be fireworks, she thought to herself. Everything was going so well, the President had been drawing large and cheering crowds everywhere they went. As she hoped for the best, Vice President Johnson's Secret Service agent jumped on top of Lyndon with instructions for Lady Bird to "Get down."

She noticed the car accelerating more and more, going so fast, she felt the car barely clearing a curve before it came to a complete stop. As she raised her heard, she could tell that they had parked at a building, and the first sign she saw said, "HOSPITAL." She writes, "Only then did I believe that this might be what it was." At the hospital, she and Nellie Connally had a long hug, for they had been through so much together. Mr. Connally had been seriously wounded, but he survived.

Lady Bird's famous encounter with Jacqueline Kennedy aboard *Air Force One* is firmly etched upon our minds. Mrs. Johnson must have winced to herself as she gazed upon Mrs. Kennedy's raspberry wool suit stained and caked with President Kennedy's blood. Thinking Mrs. Kennedy to be a dignified and reserved person, Lady Bird could never have imagined her to utter those now immortal words when it was suggested she change clothes, "I want them to see what they have done to Jack." Mrs. Johnson recalls in her diary that Mrs. Kennedy said that phrase with an "element of fierceness."

Lady Bird had long known Lyndon to be a good man in a tight spot. That must have worked to ease her mind as she rode along side him in what had to be one of the most depressing *Air Force One* flights in history. She noted in her diary that everyone was quiet and seemed to be immersed in their own thoughts. We can only imagine the thoughts Lady Bird was having. As she was sitting there, she wrote in her diary that she thought of Lyndon telling her to make sure the girls have a Secret Service agent with them. Therefore she had to be thinking about how much being propelled into the presidency would change their lives.

She was settled well into the role of vice presidential wife. Years later she recalled that time as the happiest years of her political life, even stating that she enjoyed those years better than Lyndon himself. One can easily see why she enjoyed it so much. She had been a Congressional wife for practically her whole time in Washington, and she could easily carry on the role of vice presidential wife, since Lyndon was President of the Senate. It surely crossed her mind that now she was no longer just one, in a group of one-hundred and one. As First Lady, she would be the number one woman in America, no longer able to hide in the Senate Wives club.

Something else to keep in mind, just as there were two presidents returning to Washington; so would there be two First Ladies. Following the footsteps of a glamorous and sophisticated woman like Jacqueline Kennedy would make anyone nervous. Just as Lyndon was wondering how he could survive in the shadow of JFK, Lady Bird was wondering how to weather the comparisons to Jackie and be allowed to carve out her own role as First Lady. Her dairy entry for the day after the assassination stated her and Lyndon's task would be to help the country go on living. She could never have imagined how tough that would be as the 60s unfolded. Lyndon Johnson would need his "Gentle Hand" now more than he would at any other time in his life.

ENTERING CAMELOT'S SHADOW

President Kennedy was catapulted to the realm of myth by the awful manner in which he had been struck down. Indeed, Mrs. Kennedy made sure that his 1000 days as president would be remembered as "Camelot." However, the somber truth is that much of Kennedy's legislative agenda was stuck in Congress at the time of his death. It took Lyndon Johnson's skills and Senate experience to cut taxes, obtain civil rights legislation, fight poverty, and put a man on the moon. Johnson was able to capitalize on the Kennedy mystique to persuade Congress to pass much of Kennedy's legislation. As the new President set forth with a bold agenda, so to did his wife set about to radically change the position of First Lady forever.

Liz Carpenter's appointment as press secretary marked the first time in history that a First Lady had her own press person. Carpenter's journalistic background made her simply "one of the gals" when she gave a press conference or made a special announcement. She knew first hand the world of deadlines and press pools. She put her task as simply to "help her, help him." It would not be a reach to say that Carpenter was the reason Mrs. Johnson stayed on good terms with the media.[1]

Lady Bird spent those first few weeks of her First Ladyship doing what a normal wife would be doing in her situation. She was arranging the moving of furniture to their new home, working with the out going occupant of their new house every step of the way. Granted, the average housewife would not be moving into the White House and be married to the President of the United States. Therefore Lady Bird had to worry about hiring a staff, public engagements, and finding a niche for herself since everything she did or said would make news worldwide. One can be sure Lady Bird started to worry about the clothes she wore, especially since she was following Mrs. Kennedy. However, the media was respectful to Mrs. Johnson in that they didn't hold her to the fashion standards set by her debonair predecessor.

President Johnson's past heart problems began to worry Lady Bird just a few short weeks after they took office. She overheard a lot of important people down at the ranch and could ascertain that Lyndon now had some mighty big issues to deal with, what she described as "very weighty problems." No doubt she must have been talking about Viet Nam, the Soviet Union, and civil rights. Yes, the threat of nuclear annihilation that was on her husband's mind made her start to worry more and more about his heart.

Lady Bird was very fortunate that she did not have to deal with such "weighty" matters. She turned her sights on continuing Mrs. Kennedy's preservation and restoration of the White House. Lady Bird met with long time Washington attorney Clark Clifford to discuss how to carry on the Committee for the Preservation of the White House.

The fact that Lady Bird chose this project virtually from the start is not surprising. Mrs. Kennedy had taken the time during what was a period of tremendous grieving to handwrite a letter to Lady Bird detailing what she had been doing to restore the White House in a manner befitting a Head of State. Thrust into the role of First Lady as she was, this was a simple project to continue, as it would preserve the legacy and memory of the family that was moving out.

Lady Bird's White House Diary is a wonderful tool to use when gauging the Johnson years. It is a smooth-flowing chronological account of the days in the White House that mattered most to Lady Bird. The diary is particularly helpful when you want to get a measure of the country's mood those first few dark days after the Kennedy assassination. Lady Bird wrote in her diary that the job of her and President Johnson was to help the country go on living. One gets the sense of a nation slowly coming back to life as Lady Bird reflects on her activities in late fall of 1963 and early 1964. You do get a sense that settling into her role as First Lady is taking some getting used to. She tells Nellie Connally that she feels as if she has been thrown into a role for which she has never rehearsed. That is rather odd, considering that she had been a political wife in Washington for some 30 years prior to becoming First Lady.

One can tell that Lady Bird knows her life is going to never quite be the same again. Continuity of government has long been America's hallmark, and you certainly see that quality shining through during those dark days. That is best shown by the picture of Air Force One still in the ground in Dallas, and Lyndon Johnson is taking the Presidential oath of office with both Lady Bird and Mrs. Kennedy at his side. You have to wonder if both Johnsons ever thought of achieving the presidency in this matter. If it ever crossed her mind that tragedy could force Johnson into power at any minute.

The country did indeed go on living. Just one day after President Kennedy's funeral, White House Head Usher, J.B. West came to The Elms to meet with Lady Bird. They discussed the logistics of moving furniture from The Elms to the White House. West knew what Lady Bird could fit into the family quarters of the White House, and what would have to be sent to storage. Throughout this meeting, Lady Bird's mind was on the afternoon meeting she had with Mrs. Kennedy at the White House.

This meeting took place in a private sitting room of the family residence at the White House. Lady Bird admired the strength that Jackie had summoned to get herself through this horrible tragedy. Mrs. Kennedy kept repeating, "Don't be frightened of the house—some of the happiest years of my marriage have been spent here—you will be happy here." Both of those women could never have imagined spending the week of Thanksgiving in this manner, with the Johnsons planning to move in, the Kennedys moving out. Yet, Jackie kept her grace and composure and led Lady Bird on a guided tour of the White House residence.

She told Lady Bird that she could always trust West and the White House curator, James Ketchum. If the Johnsons didn't like a particular dish or food, Jackie said for them to tell West. When telling Lady Bird about the French Chef, Rene Verdon, Jackie said, "Jack never likes those rich things that Rene does." Lady Bird wrote in her diary that neither she nor Jackie seemed to notice the present tense. Jackie asked Lady Bird to let Caroline's school carry on until the end of the year, and Lady Bird was delighted to say yes. Mrs. Kennedy led Lady Bird into her favorite room, the Yellow Room. Walking into this room, Lady Bird noticed a pair of boots and a folded flag on the table.

MOVING IN AND GOING ON

The Johnsons moved into the White House on December 7, 1963. Lady Bird, ever the serious student of history, was a little uneasy about moving into the White House on Pearl Harbor, but Lyndon insisted that that was a good time for Mrs. Kennedy. She carried in the portrait of Sam Rayburn that had hung in the Johnson family home for years. Lady Bird thought that day of how Rayburn had been present for every major milestone of the Johnson family and deeply missed him now that they needed his wise counsel more than ever. Also, she was carrying a heavy heart for the Kennedy family and saddened that the president was struck down in her home state. Of the assassination she wrote, "I realized that my sympathy must go on through the years with an increasing understanding that the world must go on, and we must go on with the world."

And go on they did. On that cold December day, Lady Bird got in a car with Liz and Bess, and Luci brought the Johnson family beagles, Him and Her to the White House in her own car. Once she drove through the gates, the reality of new role sank in. They were several newswomen waiting at the gate, and Lady Bird then knew that from now on, her every move would be news. She recorded in her diary that such scrutiny would take some getting used to, but she hoped for some private moments in the White House. A journalist by training, she understand the needs of the media, and would try to accommodate them as much as possible. Advice to Liz from newswomen was "Be available" and "Never Lie," and Mrs. Johnson so no problem with both counts.

Showing her personal touch, Lady Bird asked head usher JB West to introduce her to all the household staff. So her and Bess went around and met the maids, butlers and cleaning men that would be making the Johnsons day to day life as comfortable and simple as possible.

The Johnsons spent Christmas 1964 like any other, down at the ranch. They were able to leave Washington Christmas Eve morning since Congress passed the Foreign Aid Bill. They paid a visit to the Governor and Mrs. Connally on their way to the ranch. Once home, Lady Bird got yet another reminder that she was now in a public role. The Secret Service had installed guard houses at every gate, two signal towers, and a search light. Mrs. Johnson recorded in her diary that she would surely have to get used to the fact that her family had lost there anonymity among the vast Texas pastures.

The entire Johnson family cousins, aunts, uncles, and brothers and sisters gathered at the ranch for Christmas Eve Dinner. About fifty to seventy-five members of the press were on hand to take a family photograph, and Lyndon insisted on granting the request of a newswoman to take them on a tour of house, even with dinner on the table and ready to serve. Lady Bird tried to get him to wait by reminded him that the press would be back on Friday, but in classic LBJ manner, he gave the tour anyway.

Mrs. Johnson was able to spend New Years Eve with her family and do her favorite thing of sitting around the fire and reminiscing about the past with her kinfolk. 1964 was to be a year in which Lady Bird would find her voice and totally revolutionize the role of First Lady.

ENDNOTES

[1] Carpenter, p. 6

Chapter 6

CARVING HER NICHE INTO THE NATION

War on Poverty Gets Underway

Lady Bird began the New Year getting settling into role that had been thrust upon her. Right after the Kennedy assassination she was telling friends that she felt she was on stage for a part for which never rehearsed. Perhaps the New Year made her realize that she had to play the part. Maybe she found this ability to carry on from deep within her. After all, the lady in Dallas that fateful November day had come a long way from her days as a shy little girl in Karnack. Surely her experiences as a Congressional wife must have prepared to be the wife of the President of the United States. Someday serving as First Lady probably crossed Lady Bird's mind since Lyndon ran for the Presidency in 1960.

Mrs. Johnson sat in the gallery with Luci as Lyndon gave his first official State of the Union on January 8, 1964. The lines that grabbed Mrs. Johnson were "This Administration here and now declares unconditional war on poverty in America." She mentions in her diary that she particularly liked the line about how a thousand dollars invested in an unemployable youth today can be returned by as much as forty thousand in his lifetime.

Fighting poverty was to be the main issue Lady Bird would focus on in early 1964. Shortly after the State of the Union, Mrs. Johnson sat down with some of her staff to discuss her upcoming visit to the coal producing areas of Pennsylvania. Liz Carpenter, Mac Kilduff, and several staffers from the Area Redevelopment Administration discussed the economics of the region and showed Mrs. Johnson maps of the places she would be going to. This was typical Lady Bird. Before she went on any trip, she wanted to know everything there was to know about the place she was visiting. Liz Carpenter quoted Mrs. Johnson, "I like to get out and see the people behind the statistics." She also said she enjoyed her trips for "Its makes Lyndon's memos and working papers come alive for me."[1]

Her first major trip as First Lady helped her to achieve just that. On Saturday, January 11 1964, Mrs. Johnson set out for Wilkes-Barre and Scranton in Pennsylvania. The decline in the coal industry had hit the area hard. Forty newswomen went with her to carry this message and put a face on the War on Poverty. And what a story they got.

Lady Bird visited the Wyoming Valley Technical Institute that was helping former miners obtain skills so they could easily find other jobs. One man was learning painting because three mines had closed up on him and he told Mrs. Johnson that he thought he had "better get out of that business." One student had lost his hand in an industrial accident and was learning ceramics and he presented Mrs. Johnson with a bowl he had made. Lady Bird was pleased to learn the school offered classes in the evening and that all students were assured of a job after training.

Further bringing development to rural Pennsylvania, Lady Bird dedicated a science center at Wilkerson College. The hope is for the center to attract new businesses to the area. There were already plans to locate an RCA plant there. In her diary entry for this trip, Mrs. Johnson seemed to recognize that electronics was the wave of the future and the communities in Pennsylvania were "building their own economic bridges to the future."

To illustrate her new life as First Lady, consider this. Upon returning to the White House from the Pennsylvania trip, she had ten minutes to change and be downstairs for a Democratic National Committee reception. After receiving the 150 guest, Lyndon and Lady Bird spoke to the crowd. But rest had come; President Johnson had decided to spend the weekend at Camp David.

They were joined at Camp David by the McNamaras and Senator Russell arrived later on in the day. Lady Bird did enjoy the solitude of the presidential retreat. She wrote in her diary, "there is an insulation here that keeps you from being terribly worried about what is going on in the outside world."

Lady Bird noticed that President Johnson had begun to say grace ever since those horrific events of last November. She was happy that he realized that he needed some guidance in his job, and she is happy he is going about getting that guidance. This seems quite natural, since events of this kind make one aware of his own mortality.

The Johnsons were to host their first White House State Dinner on January 14 for the President of Italy, Signora Segnia. She was briefed by Frank Meloy on Italy's history, politics, and economics. This was the standard procedure for any state visit. She read up on the biographies of the visiting dignitaries and their delegations. She always checks the National Geographic map on the third floor of the White House to see the countries neighbors and it's "placement in the world." She recalled year later that she stills remembers where that map was.

The Italian dinner begin as any other, with cocktails in the Yellow Room. Present for these intimate occasion were just the president, First Lady, the visiting head of state and his spouse, the two ambassadors, and the chief of protocol. The exchange of gifts between President Johnson and the other head of State took place in the Yellow Room. Bess Abell recalls Lyndon telling her to spend more imagination and less taxpayer money on the gifts.

For the Italian president, the Johnsons gave a silver desk box engraved with a map of Italy and the United States and a quote from Henry Wadsworth Longfellow, "Italy remains to all, the land of dreams and a vision of delight." They also presented a 1774 letter framed in leather from Italian Philip Mazzei to Thomas Jefferson and Benjamin Franklin in response to them for asking Mazzei to come to the United States and help with wheat production and vineyards.

Once the gift exchange was over, President Johnson, Mrs. Johnson, President Segnia, and Mrs. Segnia walked down the grand staircase with a full military escort as Hail to the Chief played. After greeting the guest through a receiving line, dinner was served in the State Dining Room. When planning the guest list, Bess Abell recalled that President Johnson thought the walls of the dining room were made of elastic. He would often invite someone at the last minute, and Abell tried to find a White House staffer willing to give up their seat. An invitation to a White House State Dinner is the most coveted in the world. Abell said people would try anything to get invited. She recalled one man who told her that his wife was sick with cancer and her final wish was to attend a White House State Dinner. The Johnsons agreed to invite the couple and the woman was alive for many years after that State Dinner.

Mrs. Johnson learned from the Italian dinner that she wanted to have a personal moment of contact with each guest. In the future, she would study the guest list and learned an interesting tid-bit about the guest that she could mention to them in the receiving line. She would have an aide behind her to make sure she got the name of the guest.

Deeds, Not Words

Lady Bird looked after Lyndon. She was concerned about him for there were some nights when the president did not get home until the wee hours of the morning. Mrs. Johnson met with West and they decided that when they get word that the president would be working late, Wes would send over some sandwiches, candy, and drinks to the West Wing around nine or so. She wrote in her diary that she did this because "I'm thinking of Lyndon. And second, there are some other women's husbands there who might be hungry too."

On Thursday, January 16, Mrs. Johnson held the first of what would become her "Women Do-ers" luncheons. The idea was to showcase women who were making a difference in the country and the world. The guest included several Senate wives, the wife of the Vermont governor, and the actress Helen Hayes. Ellen Stoutenberg was the guest speaker, telling of her experiences working for the United Nations.

That evening President Johnson hosted the chairman and ranking members of Congressional committees for dinner, a total of sixty-four guest in all. Johnson went off with the men to discuss policy, and Lady Bird took the wives on a tour of the White House. She was shocked to learn that the wives of senior members of Congress had never seen the White House residence. The Lincoln Room drew the most interest, and Lady Bird pointed out the furniture that had been in use during Lincoln's tenure. However, Lincoln had actually slept in the bedroom that Mrs. Johnson is now using. Below the plaque noting Lincoln's use of the room, the ladies noticed another plaque, "In this room lived John Fitzgerald Kennedy with his wife Jacqueline during the two years, ten months, and two days he was President of the Unite States." Thus, Mrs. Johnson awoke every morning in the shadow of President Kennedy, a shadow that would linger throughout Johnson's term.

Lady Bird carried on Mrs. Kennedy's project to restore the White House to a manner befitting a Head of State, and saw it to it that the mansion showcased some of America's finest art. President Johnson signed an executive order making the position of White House Curator permanent. Mrs. Johnson requested that so the White House wouldn't "be at the whim of any First Lady." The order also created a Committee for the Preservation of the White House. On the committee were the heads of the Fine Arts Commission, National Gallery, Smithsonian Institution, and the National Park Service. The First Lady could appoint public members. Mrs. Kennedy suggested Henry Dupont, the chair of the Fine Arts Commission, and James Forbough, the head of the Painting Committee. Mrs. Johnson was happy to oblige, given the credentials of both men.

Mrs. Johnson sat down in the Queens Room with Abe Fortas, Clark Cifford, Bill Walton, Pierre Salinger, and Liz Carpenter to discuss White House preservation matters. At this meeting Clifford announced that Mrs. Kennedy had agreed to serve on the Committee for the Preservation of the White House. Lady Bird had been trying to get her to do that since November. Her hope was that Mrs. Kennedy would be the committee's "flame and fuel."

Jackie Kennedy would be a constant shadow for Mrs. Johnson during her tenure as First Lady. To her credit, Mrs. Johnson decided she was not really going to follow in anyone footsteps. She was going to blaze her own trial. Upon becoming First Lady, she said her role would emerge in deeds, not words.

THE KENNEDY LEGACY

President Kennedy's Tax Bill passed the Congress on February 26. Lady Bird and Lynda were present for the bill signing. The eleven and a half billon dollar tax cut was at the time, the largest in history. It was meant to stimulate economic growth by putting four or five extra dollars into the hands of wage earners and releasing millions of dollars from corporations into the private economy. President Johnson mentioned that it was Kennedy who originally proposed the bill.

The very evening of the bill signing, the Johnsons and the entire Cabinet went to deliver four pens used to sign the bill to Mrs. Kennedy. This seemed appropriate since Johnson had asked the entire Kennedy Cabinet to stay on. One pen was presented to Jacqueline; the other two were for Caroline and John Junior, and one for the JFK library. Secretary of State Dean Rusk presented Mrs. Kennedy with a silver tray and coffee service. Names of the Kennedy Cabinet and key advisors were engraved on the tray. Lady Bird enjoyed the company of John and Caroline.

As the Johnsons were leaving, the President stopped to say a few words to the press. He acknowledged President Kennedy's hard work on the tax bill and said the visit with Mrs. Kennedy was "very moving." That night as she went to sleep, Lady Bird remembered the inscription on the tray giving to Mrs. Kennedy, "In memory of three shining years together."

The Johnsons spent time with some more Kennedys later on that same week. They visited the home of Joe and Rose Kennedy, the patriarch and matriarch of the Kennedy family at their home in Palm Beach, Florida. Lady Bird was impressed that Rose was holding up so well giving the fact that she had lost a son and her husband was an invalid due to a severe stroke. Rose let it be known that she was grateful to President Johnson for all the support he had showed the family after that terrible tragedy in Dallas.

Lady Bird was to meet with Jacqueline Kennedy at eleven on the morning of Friday, February 29 to discuss the White House preservation project. Before the meeting, Mrs. Johnson studied all there was to know about the Committee for the Preservation of the White House, the Painting Committee, as well as the Fine Arts

Committee. She also read again Mrs. Kennedy's handwritten memo to her regarding preservation.

So, on that cold bitter morning, Lady Bird met with Mrs. Kennedy in her Georgetown home. Over coffee, Mrs. Johnson went over with Kennedy every detail she could think of concerning the preservation committee. She told Mrs. Kennedy that the committee should have the following regular members: the head of the National Park Service, George Hertzog, the White House Head Usher, J.B. West, White House curator Jim Ketchum, Bill Walton, director of the National Gallery of Art, and the Director of the Smithsonian, Dillon Ripley. Mrs. Kennedy agreed to be a public member and Lady Bird told her that she hoped Kennedy would be the catalyst to inspire the committee to keep going. Before leaving, Mrs. Johnson presented Kennedy with the first four of the Kennedy half dollar, one for her, one for each of the children, and one for Rose Kennedy.

After what had to be a rather stressful meeting with Mrs. Kennedy, Lady Bird got a pleasant surprise. John and Nellie Connally were up from Texas for a visit. When the time came for the Conallys plane to leave, the flight was canceled due to the snow. They were then settled into the Queens Room and Walter Jenkins came over for dinner. Lady Bird wrote of the evening, "I had the same delightful feeling you get at the ranch when the river rises and you cannot get across, and the only thing to do is to relax." She must have no doubt been relieved that Lyndon was getting some much needed rest from the burdens of the presidency.

Word came that the King of Greece had passed away and it was decided that Lady Bird would represent the United States at the funeral. Both Johnson called President Truman and invited him along, who was by this time 80 years old, but still going strong. Mrs. Johnson told Truman that the trip would be much more meaningful if he came along, and the former president agreed. A delegation of prominent Americans of Greek descent accompanied Mrs. Johnson and Truman.

On the flight over, Lady Bird asked Truman about his policy toward Greece, known to history as the Truman Doctrine. He said it was simply an extension of the Marshall Plan that had helped Europe rebuild after World War II. She also sought his advice of what a presidential wife should do. He told her, "Protect him. Don't let people use you. If people bring you some sort of proposition they want you to take to the president, it is all right to tell him, but if you have any doubts about them be sure and tell him that." He related that when he failed to rely on Mrs. Truman's judgment, he always regretted it later.

Knowing Mrs. Johnson's deep interest in history, it was a real treat to have Truman along with her. She asked him about his life since the White House. He said he was doing a series of lectures: one on periods of hysteria in American history, one on the presidency, and one on the relationship between the Executive and Legislative branches of government. Truman's mentioning of hysteria sparked a conversation between he and Mrs. Johnson on the Salem Witch Trials and Joe McCarthy.

Prince Michael greeted the American delegation once *Air Force One* landed in Greece. The prince told Truman that his grandfather had been aide-de-camp to General Grant. Truman answered, "Young man, as far as that little lady over there is concerned, and me too, your grandfather was on the wrong side." Seeing that Prince Michael was somewhat taken aback, Lady Bird explained that "although we have had our wounds and suffered deeply, the years have taught us that if we are going to be one nation, we got to be united and forget our hostilities." She had hoped that would teach the prince a lesson in regards to the current tensions between Greece and Cyprus. At this point in her diary she recorded, "Really the more I see of the rest of the world, the prouder I am of the United States."

Truman joined Mrs. Johnson at the informal supper Queen Frederika hosted to receive the funeral guest. Upon arriving at the palace, Lady Bird was told the queen wanted a private audience with her. She recorded in her diary that the queen came across as trite but Mrs. Johnson expressed her sympathy and said it must have been said for Frederika to return to Greece from the United States to find the king so ill.

The funeral served as a family reunion for European royalty but Mrs. Johnson was not shy and went up to people she had just met once, or not at all, and simply introduced herself. On the way back to the hotel after the burial, Truman made some interesting remarks to Mrs. Johnson. He said the only reason FDR picked him to be Vice President was because Roosevelt didn't want anyone who would follow him into the presidency that would do a better job than he had done. Mrs. Johnson was no doubt pleased to hear Truman say, "I want Lyndon Johnson to do well. I know he's going to be a great President. You know I've been for him all these years." She liked that fact that Truman treated everyone the same, from "Kings to elevator boys." Her diary entry for the Greek trip concludes, "I must say that being with President Truman those days has been one of the big pluses of this period in my life."

In the midst of sorrow, there is always joy. The Johnsons celebrated Lynda's twentieth birthday on March 20. Her parents gave her money and Zephyr made an angel food cake with pink icing. Everyone was looking forward to the big Democratic dinner to be held that night. Lady Bird was excited to have a chance to wear her red ball gown and Lynda was pleased to get a pink crepe dress for the occasion.

Just to show how unpredictable life in the White House can be, in the middle of Lynda's birthday celebrations and the preparations for the Democratic dinner,

Pierre Salinger informed President Johnson that he was resigning as press secretary and moving out to California to run for the Senate. George Reedy was in the hospital, but that didn't stop Lyndon from calling him and asking him to be his next press secretary. Of all the Kennedy staffers, Mrs. Johnson felt closest to Salinger. She wrote in her diary that his resignation "leaves a big uncertainty in my own thinking."

Since the Democratic dinner at the armory was held the day after Saint Patrick's Day, the room was decked out in green and white Irish decorations. Shamrocks, top hats, and potatoes were everywhere and Lady Bird wrote that it all reminded you of one person, President Kennedy. She also recorded in her diary that Lyndon's speech for the event was "quite competent, but not sparkling."

Lynda's birthday was recognized when a silver donkey with a green top hat and green bow tie carrying a shamrock that said "Happy Birthday Lynda" was presented to her along with a thirty-five pound cake complete with twenty pink candles. They event had some sentimental value for the Johnsons since it was in honor of the Congressional Class of 1936. President Johnson, of course joined the Congress in 1935, but he always included in the class of 1936. They were also happy to see so many donors from Texas including thirty-five from Johnson's old Congressional district.

Given the Irish decorations, the Salinger resignation, and the lack of attendance by any member of the Kennedy family, Lady Bird wrote that it "All helped to evoke that curious mood." It proves how strongly the Johnsons felt the Kennedy shadow upon them. The fact that President Johnson evoked Kennedy's memory and in order to achieve much of his agenda, yet try to serve as his own man made for an interesting paradox that would haunt Johnson throughout his presidency.

THE SOUTH HAS HITCHED IT'S WAGON TO THE STARS

Mrs. Paul Mellon arrived at the White House on March 19 to tour the gardens with Lady Bird. She was the daughter-in-law of former Treasury Secretary Andrew Mellon and donated the National Art Gallery and many of its artifacts to the government. Mrs. Mellon is a well known authority on gardens and planting and helped Mrs. Kennedy with the restoration of the Rose Garden. Lady Bird is now overseeing Mellon's transformation of the East Garden into "a very dainty, feminine garden." Mrs. Johnson proposed renaming the garden the Jacqueline Kennedy Garden and her husband happily agreed. She also got approval from Clark Clifford who told her to check with the Director of the National Park

Service, George Hertzog and the chair of the Fine Arts Commission, Bill Walton. Both men saw no problem with naming the garden in honor of Mrs. Kennedy, and all that was left was for Mrs. Johnson to call Kennedy for her approval.

Kennedy at first turned down the offer. She was of the strong conviction that presidential wives deserve no recognition, that it was President Kennedy who had done all of the work. However, Mrs. Kennedy was happy to see Mellon continuing the work on the garden and said, "Well if she wants to scratch my initials on a tree, or put it on a plaque, ever so little, underneath some bench."

Early on the morning of March 24, Liz Carpenter and some thirty odd reporters departed Washington with Lady Bird for Alabama for a tour of NASA's Space Flight Center in Huntsville. Shortly after 9, Mrs. Johnson arrived and was greeted by the Director of NASA, the Space Flight Center director, and other local dignitaries. Of particular interest to Mrs. Johnson was seventy year old Mary Derrberry, a space center employee.

At the welcoming ceremony, Lady Bird spoke of how Lyndon had authored the Space Act of 1958 and said, "By osmosis, a lot of his interest had rubbed off on me." Furthermore, she was pleased that women compromised twenty percent of the payroll at the Marshall center. Some were even aerospace engineers.

Always wanting to highlight the South's present, instead of it's past she said, "The South has hitched it's wagon to the stars." She was pleased that the South was leading the way in the race to the moon. Mrs. Johnson got a complete look at the Saturn rocket which was being designed to someday put a man on the moon. She saw an astronaut's suit and a small craft that would land on the moon.

A rather humorous incident occurred when Mrs. Johnson observed a test firing of Saturn's eight engine cluster. At the count of zero, there was a loud earth shaking boom that was followed by two minutes of flame pouring out from the engines. Jim Well put his arm tight around Lady Bird the second the engine went off, and a photograph caught the moment. Liz Carpenter joked that the caption should read, "Lady Bird, after this is over, let's you and me go out and have a drink." Here day in Alabama ended with an awards ceremony and a reception with local leaders hosted by Mrs. Webb and Mrs. Van Braum.

On April 8, the Johnsons attended the funeral of famed General Douglas McArthur. Lady Bird at an interesting exchang at the occasion. Robert Kennedy came up to her and said, "We seem to always be meeting at funerals." She stood next to him during the funeral procession and at one point he leaned over and said, "You're doing a wonderful job. Everybody says so." Then after a brief pause, he said, "And so is your husband."

After the ceremony in the rotunda, the Johnsons had the McCarthy family over at the White House for tea. Mrs. Johnson said that she didn't know them well, "But the whole country had really known him well. And this had been a very dignified departure from life, a most respectful good-bye."

After that, Mrs. Johnson prepared for the next day, in which was going to deliver a major speech. She was the guest speaker at a lunch to commemorate the first anniversary of the Eleanor Roosevelt Memorial Foundation. Hester Provenson worked with her on the speech for two hours.

The next morning she flew commercial along with Liz Carpenter and Bess Abell from her staff. Before the main lunch with 2,000 guests that paid twelve dollars each, Lady Bird greeting guest at a reception for those that gave a thousand dollars. Eleanor Roosevelt's granddaughter, Anna Hoffman joined her as the received the guest made up of the charity and financial elite of New York City.

Hoffman spoke at the lunch and Mrs. Johnson was moved as she read the last letter her grandma had written to her. The Ambassador to the United Nations, Adalai Stevenson introduced Mrs. Johnson. Though she didn't relish the idea of having to speak she wrote in her diary, "Having lived those years with the Roosevelt regime, I really felt like talking about them." She recalled being moved when Eleanor attended a luncheon held in 1939 by the Seventy-Fifth Congress Club to help raise money to buy a little boy a wheel chair. Lady Bird told the crowd, "Only one person would benefit, but where else do you start except with one person?. Mrs. Roosevelt was always ready to start. Anyone person was important to her."

This was a great moment for Mrs. Johnson. The thought never entered her mind that day in 1939 that she would same day be First Lady and speak at a benefit in memory of Mrs. Roosevelt. In her speech, Lady Bird went on to praise Roosevelt for standing up for her convictions saying, "She was never afraid to speak up against wrong, no matter who many brickbats it brought down on her head."

Then it was back to the real world of modern Washington. Upon arriving back at the White House, she discovered that Lyndon had called the parties involved in the rail road stike for a meeting to help them reach a settlement. Knowing her husband well, she was not surprised to find him bold enough to jump into the middle of a dispute that had been festering for years. President Johnson didn't arrive back in the residence that night until midnight.

He did not return empty handed. Five hours of pressure from Johnson got both sides to agree to postpone the strike for fifteen days in order to extend the negotiations. The meetings were held next door to the White House in the Old Executive Office Building so Johnson could keep close watch on the proceedings. He went to one of the sessions and mentioned that both the Secretary of Labor and

Council of Economic Advisors said that a strike would cripple the economy and thus his presidency. The Johnson treatment had worked. When the president agreed to pressure Congress to allow carriers the freedom to set rates and to direct the IRS to grant liberal depreciation allowances on tunnel and bridge construction, the strike ended.

Lady Bird had watched the negotiations closely and was praying for a settlement. She got word on the evening of April 23 to tune into the David Brinkley show. She was pleased to see Lyndon with the rail road officials announcing the settlement live on television. When President Johnson arrived back at the White House she wrote that he was "on that Olympic peak."

April was just as exciting for Lady Bird. She honored Eleanor Roosevelt and hosted famed poet Carl Sandburg and his brother-in-law the photographer Edward Steichen. She was impressed that Sandburg was still going strong at the age of 85, and made a point to read a collection of his poems before his visit.

Since Sandburg was a renowed Lincoln biographer, she took him to the Lincoln Room. He signed two of his Lincoln works that is part of the White House library. She tried to point out the objects in the room that was connected to Lincoln, but she wrote that was difficult, "because he did all of the talking."

She wrote that both Sandburg and Steichen to be pleasant company. Luci was able to get Sandburg to sing a book of poems signed and Liz Carpenter was enamored by being in his presence. Lady Bird enjoyed Sandburg's sense of humor, especially his joke and Steichen's beard, he wanted "to raise a beard and he didn't know what kind he wanted, and so he decided he would copy one after the Prophet Isaiah." From the Rose Garden, President Johnson took both men into the Cabinet Room to see the rail road stroke negotiations because Johnson wanted them to see "men who can throw several million people out of work."

After joining the president at the welcoming ceremony for King Hussein of Jordan and opening the Department of Agriculture's Food and Home Fair for Economics, Lady Bird attended her first Senate Ladies Red Cross Luncheon as a guest. Of course, she had to been to fifteen of these lunches, but it felt different going as a First Lady and not a Senate wife. She enjoyed herself and Mrs. Dirksen presented her with a bracelet charm that had the Senate seal on one side and the date and an inscription on the other. Mrs. Johnson wrote of the event in her diary the "sense of drive that prevailed when Lyndon was in the Senate, and which always by osmosis transferred itself to the Senate Ladies and to me, seemed somewhat missing."

Mrs. Johnson did what other Americans always do that time of year; she signed her tax returns just in time to meet the deadline. She then changed into her yellow chiffon evening dress for the state dinner in honor of King Hussein. One notable dinner guest was J. Edgar Hoover. Lady Bird recorded in her diary that he "never goes to affairs of this sort but has always seemed to have a very real respect and personal liking for Lyndon."

During the dancing afterwards, Mrs. Johnson heard an interesting exchange between Secretary of Agriculture Orville Freeman and his wife. When Mrs. Freeman wanted to dance, he told her, if she testified in his place in front of the Appropriations committee in the morning, they could dance. Dr. Allan Kelvic, a dinner guest told Lady Bird that Hussein had started a program in Jordan to immunize every child against polio. She said in her diary that she likes all she hears about the King and likes how he connects with his people.

Just as Lady Bird would like to advance her own trips, she would like to experience White House events through the eyes of a guest. Just to show her concern for how White House events are carried out, she quotes a society columnist comments on the Jordan dinner in her diary. She was happy the columnist reported favorably on the dinner and liked the review she herself received, "but it was Mrs. Johnson who seemed to enjoy the music the most. She tapped one gilt-shod foot and kept time with the rythmatic drumming of her finger on her program."

On Thursday April 16, Lady Bird finally got to have dinner with Barbara Walsh, author of *Rich Nations and Poor Nations*. The president and Dr. Willis Hurst joined them. Her book the attention of the president, and he used it as a blueprint for his war on poverty. Walsh had been living at the White House and wrote speeches and drafted memos to the president. In such settings, President Johnson usually does all the talking, but Lady Bird was surprised that he just listened as Walsh talked. The First Lady couldn't help but notice that Walsh thought that anything was possible and was always full of ideas.

Walsh had the idea that money saved from base closings could be used for urban renewal programs. She believed that America possessed enough natural resources and inventiveness that would build a new society and offer more for everyone. Giving Lyndon Johnson's plans to build a "Great Society," it is easy to see why he was attracted to Walsh's ideas.

Spring of 1964 was a time in which Johnson and many other political leaders believed that we could afford both the War on Poverty and the Vietnam War. Remember, at this time, the war was not making front page news and Johnson had not escalated American involvement in Vietnam.

As every spring, the American Society of Newspaper Editors gathered in Washington. The Johnsons hosted the twelve hundred editors to a White House reception on Friday, April 17. President Johnson had the forty editors from Texas over for dinner the evening before.

Lady Bird was thankful the weather had turned out nice so all the guest could go out onto the South Lawn and the Rose Garden. She made a few opening remarks then handed it over to Lynda who did a superb job delivering her lines. President Johnson then spoke about Medicare, civil rights, and the war on poverty. One line Lady Bird liked was about "turning tax eaters into tax payers." Speaking of the Cold War he said, "we must love each other or we must die." Mrs. Johnson recorded in her diary that during the next decade, the leadership of the United States could very well determine the destiny of the world.

As the throng of editors crowded in the East Room and State Dining Room for food and dancing, Luci arrived to help the rest of her family greed the guest. Lady Bird was thrilled to see her first editor, Daniel Hall, who was at the Daily Texan back in 1934 when she got her degree in journalism. She talked with George Healy of New Orleans who told her all about the G.P. Healy paintings that was in possession of the White House. Also present were Mr. and Mrs. Joseph Pulitzer Junior whom Lady Bird was impressed to meet. The Johnsons finished off the reception by spending two hours dancing with as many guest as possible.

Lady Bird found herself doing what all mothers do. She comforted Luci when she had to tell Bernie Rosenbach good-bye. Since he was heading off with the Navy, both he and Luci thought it wise that they separate. When he returned back that December, they would meet and either agree to start seeing each other again or even get engaged. Bernie stopped by to tell Mrs. Johnson herself, then he went in to see Lyndon. She appreciated that because she wanted him to "share in some of our girl's heartaches, as well as their joys." It can be said that throughout her public role, Lady Bird never gave up her private role as mother and wife.

Never one to shrink from bold moves, such as promoting civil rights in Southern states, Lady Bird decided to host a White House reception in honor of the Daughters of the American Revolution. The group had faced charges of racism in the past when they refused to let Dinah Washington sing in Constitution Hall and Eleanor Roosevelt hosted a concert for her at the Lincoln Memorial. However, Lady Bird admired the Daughters for their scholarships, schools in Appalachia, and national monument preservation. She recorded in her diary, that if you call people bigots long enough, "the human reaction would be to begin to defend yourself and harden in attitude."

Over two hundred members of the Daughters attended the reception, the first held for them in the White House since 1953. The president of the organization presented a pair of white gloves to Lady Bird. Johnson enjoyed the event and recorded in her diary, "I do not remember a more friendly group or one more responsive to being in this house."

ENDNOTE

[1] Carpenter, p. 74

Chapter 7

THE LAST CAMPAIGN

THEY MAKE THEIR MEN WITH STEEL

As the spring of 1964 went on, Lyndon Johnson had his eyes set on the upcoming campaign. He had been receiving polls that showed his popularity at 77% nationally though he had a 13% disapproval rating in the South.

To begin to lay the groundwork for a campaign and to get his agenda made known to the public, Johnson set out on a trip that would take him to Illinois, Indiana, Ohio, Pennsylvania, and West Virginia. The goal was to highlight his plans to handle poverty, unemployment, and civil rights. Some of the most poorest areas of the Appalachian region would receive national media coverage thanks to Johnson's visit.

Lady Bird went with him for she always liked to see the people behind the statistics of White House policy proposals. South Bend, Indiana had suffered a major blow when Studebaker closed its plant there right before Christmas in 1963. As a result, 8,700 people suddenly found themselves out of work. This stop was on the itinerary to show an example of how a community can recover from economic disasters.

Always one for a dramatic entry, the Johnsons landed on the playground of South Bend's Cline School and were greeted by some fifteen thousand well wishers. All struggled to get close to the Johnsons in some way. They toured a school for non-traditional students that needed to learn new job skills so they could re-enter the workforce. Mrs. Johnson was happy to meet one lady who was a typist but was learning computers so she could get a better job. The First Lady was particularly thrilled to see a practical nursing class for she knew how hard it was to find care for an ill or elderly family member.

There was a crowd waiting once the Johnsons made their way out of the school's back door. People were climbing trees and goal posts to get a good view of the President and First Lady. Lady Bird was a bit nervous at the size of the crowd, but she wrote in her diary , "the best way to behave in such situations is to be very calm and walk quickly, smiling and shaking as many hands as possible."

But, the Johnson were not alone in facing those huge crowds. They had with them, Secretary of Labor Willard Wirtz, Secretary of Commerce Luther Hodges, Secretary of Health, Education, and Welfare, Anthony Celebreze, and Undersecretary of Commerce, Franklin D. Roosevelt, Junior. Along the way, the Johnsons were greeted by local politicians and Congressman as well as the governors of each state they visited. Also along with the Johnsons was David McDonald, president of the United Steelworkers.

A stop was made in Pittsburgh so President Johnson could attend the National Convention of the League of Women Voters. Willard Wirtz was the scheduled speaker, but the night before, Wirtz had informed the League that President Johnson would be joining him.

Johnson urged the thirteen hundred delegates to fight the war on poverty for women have children and grand-children that they all want to see grow up and live in a more prosperous world. Lady Bird spoke to them and thanked them for their efforts to increase voter participation and voter education.

Next, the Johnsons made their way to the local steelworkers headquarters so Lyndon could address the union members. Lady Bird was surprised to see a quarter of a million people gathered along the streets to watch the presidential motorcade pass through. She recorded in her diary that this is when she begin to realize that Lyndon had nationwide appeal, writing that he "captured the imaginations of the great masses of eastern industrial cities to a far greater degree than we had realized."

Johnson switched to an open car and had to make three unscheduled stops and speak to crowds with a bull horn while standing on the truck of the car. He delivered his standard message on the war on poverty, unemployment and civil rights. Then Lady Bird climbed on the trunk and said a few words, thinking to herself to wear flat shoes for campaigning.

If the trip seemed liked a political outing, the event at the union hall confirmed it. Steelworkers president David McDonald introduced President Johnson and said, "the union shall do all of the down-to-earth work that is possible to elect you this November." Lady Bird recorded in her diary that moment as being the "first really outspoken assumption that Lyndon is running." As she spoke to the union members, she looked out at their faces and thought of each one of their personal stories and she used that line from Carl Sandburg, "They make their steel with men."

Then the trip took the Johnsons from the industrial to the rural. Indeed, the whole purpose of the war on poverty was to somehow find a way to bring the prosperity of the industrial cities to the rural areas of America. To show the rest of the nation the needs of rural Appalachia, the Johnsons took a helicopter from Huntington, West Virginia to the eastern Kentucky city of Inez in Martin County. Lady Bird couldn't help but notice the change of scenery from Pittsburg. She wrote in her diary, "We flew over beautiful spring-green mountains dotted with dogwood, the hill-side pockmarked here and there by the mouths of small mines."

She also noticed the streams and dirt roads all the way along the mountainside. The isolation of mountains had pulled the locals in and seemed to off no way out. Many of the mines were closed, leaving whole families with no source of income. Such was the case of Tom Fletcher. He had lost his job as a miner, and worked in a saw mill just three or four months out of the year. His total 1963 income was just four hundred dollars. The Johnsons and their entourage had to cross Rock Castle Creek on a handmade suspension bridge to get to the Fletcher home.

The Fletchers and their eight children lived in a three room tarpaper home. Two of the children had dropped out of school and Lady Bird noticed Mrs. Fletcher looked like the years of poverty had left her tired and worn. Mrs. Johnson met the local storeowner who mad a living to support her four children since her husband was too ill to work. When asked by Lady Bird what the area needed most the storeowner was quick to answer, "Jobs, we need a business or a factory to come in here." She also said they needed a hospital since the closest one was in Louisa, an hour away, and often enough they didn't have enough beds. That made Lady Bird remember that Chief Justice Fred Vinson was from Louis and she wrote in her diary, "So, you can't say this part of the country doesn't raise strong men."

President Johnson sat on the front porch and talked with Mr. Fletcher about how they live on four hundred dollars a month and how to make the kids stay in school. The picture of Lyndon talking on the front porch with Fletcher got nationwide media coverage. Lady Bird admitted that the visit was staged, but she said it was the only way to get the story of Appalachia out to the rest of the country. She found the people to decent and caring and hoped a way out could be found for them.

The last stop in Kentucky was a tour of a possible way out. Both Johnsons visited the Mayo State Vocational School in Paintsville. They were able to see a lathe shop, a hairdressing class, and an automobile shop. Lady Bird and reporters

France Lewine and Helen Thomas wished they had time to take advantage of the beauty salon. Nonetheless, Mrs. Johnson was pleased to see women learning a skill they could turn into a paycheck.

President Johnson gave a speech in the Court House square then took the helicopter back to Huntington, West Virginia. There, he had a two hour meeting with Governor Barron of West Virginia, Governor Welsh of Indiana, Governor Breathitt of Kentucky, and a representative of Governor Scranton of Pennsylvania. They discussed the three billon dollar Appalachian recovery plan. Before boarding the plane back to Washington, President Johnson gave a speech in which he stressed the main themes of the day, the war on poverty, unemployment, and civil rights.

I Cannot Return to the White House

The weekend of April 25 found the Johnsons entertaining old friends at the White House. Texas historian and professor, Frank Dotre came with his wife, and President Truman stopped by that Saturday. Someone mentioned during lunch that Republicans accused Truman of making foreign policy decisions in the dark. That prompted Truman to tell how he made the decision to drop the atomic bomb. He said the decision was made when the generals told him that an invasion of Japan would cost between 200,000-250,000 American lives. Truman said he made every decision that way. He would get the best advice possible, weigh his options, and make up his mind. Lady Bird was pleased to have Truman back at the White House for she had a special place in her heart for him since the trip to Greece.

Ever the practical one, Mrs. Johnson decided to accomplish two things at once. That evening she took Mrs. Dotre on a tour of the State Floor and used the opportunity to learn about various White House artifacts before the May 7 meeting of the Art Committee. She enjoyed telling Dorte all about the Monet paintings donated by the Kennedy family, the Waterford chandelier, and the Savonnerie rug.

Monday April 27 was a big day for Lady Bird. She had coffee that morning in the Yellow Room with Madame Indira Gandhi. Joining them were Gandhi's cousin and Mrs. Dean Rusk. Mrs. Johnson wrote in her diary that she found communicating with Gandhi rather difficult, despite the fact that she spoke fluent English. Mrs. Rusk attempted to bridge the gap by invoking topics of conversation. Lady Bird was able to discuss the trip she made to India in 1963 and the health of Jawaharbal Nehru.

Later that day, Lady Bird went to Georgetown to meet with Jacqueline Kennedy. She wrote in her diary that she went "with apology, hesitant to trespass on sadness, feeling like an intruder." Lady Bird wished to have Mrs. Kennedy at the White House on May 7 for the preservation committee meeting. Jackie held firm, "Lady Bird, but I cannot return to the White House." She then asked Kennedy if she would send a note to guide the committee members as they started back up again. But, she said, "Can't you just tell them for me that I send my best wishes." While turning down the invitation to the White House, Kennedy also said, "You know, every place I go reminds me of all the places we lived. We lived all over Georgetown." Being a wife and mother, Lady Bird understood and didn't press the issue any further.

Mrs. Johnson was able to cheer Mrs. Kennedy up a little. She brought with her the Boudin fabric Kennedy had ordered last summer. It was the type that Jefferson or Monore would likely have ordered for the East Room, and both ladies were please with the way it had turned out.

Johnson also brought with her a picture of the East Garden which was to become the Jacqueline Kennedy Garden. Mrs. Kennedy was pleased of the progress of her renovation efforts, and Lady Bird left with a feeling that Kennedy was satisfied, but still Lady Bird wished she could do more for her.

Mrs. Johnson attended the Congressional Club's annual breakfast in honor of the First Lady. She had been many times before as a Congressional wife. A thousand women packed the Sheraton Park ballroom as the Marine Band played. Mrs. Johnson had wanted to greet as many guests as possible but there was such a bright spotlight on her as she made her way to the head table, that she could hardly see at all.

When it was her turn to speak, Mrs. Johnson said, "Coming here is familiar territory to me, a little like coming to a family reunion. I remember my first Congressional breakfast, in 1938, when your guest of honor was Eleanor Roosevelt, and since then, I have been back every time, with a constituent, the most important word in our vocabulary." She left the breakfast still wanting some personal connection with the ladies, because she knew how important this breakfast was to them. However, when she went back to the Sheraton that evening so the President could speak to the Democratic Women's Conference, Lady Bird was glad that all she had to do was take a bow.

On May 6, Lady Bird hosted a lunch at the White House in honor of the Senate Ladies Red Cross Unit. Bess Abell had the idea to set the one hundred and thirty guest at twelve tables, and used every piece of White House china—from Washington to Eisenhower. Each table had a different centerpiece, which made for good conversation pieces. The rule for White House china is that when there is not enough to serve one hundred guests for a State Dinner, it is time for the current administration to order china. The Johnsons had to order china in 1968 that featured an eagle in the center with wildflowers around the border.

Mrs. Johnson received the Senate ladies in the Green Room, seventy-one wifes of current Senators, and thirty-one wives of former Senators. She was pleased to see the wives of the "old greats," Mrs. Alben Barkley, Mrs. Millard Tydings, Mrs. Tom Connally, and Mrs. Estes Kefauver. It especially made Lady Bird happy to see her friends from the old Spanish class, Grace Dodd, Bethine Church, and Abigail McCarthy.

After lunch, Mrs. Johnson gave a short speech about the first First Lady to live in the White House, Abigail Adams. Next, the ladies gathered in the East Room to watch Helen Hayes perform in A. E. Hotchner's play, *The White House*. It went over quite well, and Lady Bird wrote in her diary that it was one of "the best entertainments I've ever seen here." Once the play was over, President Johnson dropped in and called the ladies "the jewels" of the Senators and said Lady Bird is always happiest when she is among them.

With one big event down, Lady Bird set her eyes on another big event. She was hosting her first meeting of the White House Preservation Committee on May 7. She was thrilled that her old friend, Alice Brom came to stay at the White House the night before the meeting, bringing with her two paintings. One was a portrait of George Washington by Sully and the other was a Winslow Homer watercolor, "The Surf at Prout's Neck." She was pleased to have both these paintings in time for the committee meeting, and happy to acquire a Homer so early in her term.

With Lady Bird feeling anxious, the Preservation of the White House Committee convened at 10:30 the next morning in the Yellow Oval Room. Mrs. Johnson was able to show the committee a silver coffee urn used by John Adams and a sample of the fabric being used to make new drapes for the East Room. White House Head Usher J. B. West was empowered by the group to look into getting duplicate rugs for the Green Room, Blue Room, and Red Room. The concern is that the antiques rugs are being used for every event, and the committee worried they would get damaged or eventually wear out. Lady Bird considered the meeting productive, and thus a success.

Next, Lady Bird hosted an afternoon tea for members of the art world. The guest belonged to either the Fine Arts Committee, the Library Committee, or the Advisory Committee. Mrs. Johnson was able see Anne Ford, the former wife of Henry Ford II and Charles Francis Adams, a member of the John Adams family. After being received in the Green Room, the guest gathered in the Blue Room.

Each one was presented with a list of what the White House had acquired since Mrs. Kennedy's last meeting with them in December 1962.

Lady Bird spoke to the group and thanked them for their work to preserve such an important symbol of American democracy. She told them she wished they could all see the look on the faces of the tourist as they make way through the White House. She found the group to be extremely pleased as she took them from room to room. In her diary entry for the event, she says her two favorite paintings are the ones of Thomas Jefferson and Benjamin Franklin.

LEAVING ALL CARES BEHIND

Lady Bird was able to get away to Huntland, the Virginia retreat of Mr. and Mrs. George Brown. She described the surroundings as the kind that "evoke for me the thought of leaving all cares behind."

Amongst nature, Lady Bird took a walk to think about her husband's options for the upcoming election. After her walk, she called for Lyndon's team of physicians to join her to discuss whether the president's health permitted him to serve a full term or not. While waiting for the arrival of the doctors, Lady Bird wrote her husband a nine page letter detailing the situation as she saw it.

She concluded that Lyndon should run despite all the hardships the family will face by continuing in the public eye and the implications to the President's health. Lady Bird felt that her husband couldn't handle the lonely hours down at the Ranch if he does not have anything to do but "overseeing the cattle, and maybe making a few lectures." She cites the disappointment among his staff and the Democratic Party if he didn't run and she thought they would all have the feeling that President Johnson had let them down.

In her diary entry discussing whether or not the President should run, Mrs. Johnson makes an interesting remark. She wrote that if he runs now then in "February or March 1968, if the Lord lets him live that long, announce that he won't be a candidate for reelection." She felt that by then, "the juices of life" in him would have run their course so the Johnsons could "live the rest of our days quietly." Once the doctors arrive, they all agreed that the President should run.

It is not surprising that Mrs. Johnson felt that her husband should only serve one term. From her diary entries it is clear she was concerned about Lyndon's health throughout his Presidency. Also, she felt the strain of public life herself and was looking forward to living a carefree life in solitude at the Ranch. For now, life as First Lady had to continue and she should be there to be a calm and reassuring gentle hand to her husband as he bore the weight of the world on his shoulders.

IT DON'T HURT TO DREAM

Lady Bird visited Kentucky on May 21 to once again bring poverty to the attention of the American people. She loved the names of the communities she drove through, Cumberland Plateau, Troublesome Creek, Lick Branch School, and Quicksand. She was on her way to Warshoal Branch to visit the family of Arthur Robertson, who had seven children.

The party stopped near a creek and Lady Bird's escort for the day, Breathitt County Schools Superintendent Marie Turner told Lady Bird that the Robertson place was a mile up the creek. That didn't stop Johnson who simply put on her black boots and led her entourage up the hill to the three-room home of the Robertsons.

Mrs. Johnson was delighted to see the entire Robertson family waiting on the front porch to greet her. Their only daughter, Judy Ann gave her a bunch of red and gold flowers. Lady Bird found Mr. Robertson easy to talk to as he explained to her how he used a seven-hundred dollar government grant to prepare his home for winter, build a privy, and dig a well. With assistance from the Agriculture Department, he was able to grow three-fifths of an acre of tobacco. That was his only cash crap and he worked part time for the Unemployed Parents Program planting pine trees at Stray Branch.

Lady Bird wrote in her diary that part of the purpose for the trip was to show how the millions of dollars sent to Kentucky since 1961 can be used for public works, school lunches, and job training "without destroying the character and self-reliance of American citizens."

Next Lady Bird made her way to Lick Branch School, a one-room school house that reminded her of Fern School in Karnack, right down to the pot-bellied stove in the middle of the room. She had lunch with the children which cost ten cents but was free to those who could not afford it. The children performed a puppet show for Mrs. Johnson, "The Little Red Hen." She then presented the school with a flag that had flown over the capitol and Johnson joined all the students in the Pledge of Allegiance. The highlight of the day, however, was when Mrs. Johnson threw the switch to the electric lights that had just been installed at the school. Now, students would not have to be dismissed early in the winter when it gets dark in the afternoons.

The final event of the day was the dedication of a new gymnasium at Breathitt High School in Jackson, Kentucky. Lady Bird was following the footsteps of Eleanor Roosevelt who had dedicated the original gymnasium in 1938. Indeed, three graduates were present that had been at Mrs. Roosevelt's dedication. Mrs.

Johnson was impressed with the new gymnasium that was one of a hundred and eighty-eight federally funded public works projects in Cumberland area. As the day ended and Mrs. Johnson left, she kept thinking about what Mrs. Robertson had told her, "It don't hurt to dream."

A Life of Contrast

A lover of history, Lady Bird was happy to be First Lady on May 23 when she joined her husband for the dedication of the George Marshall Research Library at the VMI. They were joined by Dean Rusk, the Achesons, and Senator Byrd. As the president inspected the Cadet Honor Guard Company, Lady Bird felt sorry for those "poor dear boys" for having to wear those wool uniforms in the summer heat.

Once inside the library for a tour, the Johnsons met up with President Eisenhower, Mrs. Marshall, and Governor Harrison of Virginia. General Marshall had passed away in 1959, and Lady Bird thought, "He was a man whose character has seldom been equaled in our government's service."

Marshall's old friend, General Omar Bradley was the master of ceremonies. He told Mrs. Johnson shortly before the ceremony, "This is one of the twenty-two things I'm doing because I think they're good to. Of course, my heart is in this more than the others."

Lady Bird wrote in her diary that Eisenhower and Johnson gave the best speeches she ever heard them make. She was able to meet at least three cadets from Texas and several cadets escorted her throughout the day. Mrs. Johnson couldn't help but think of what a Civil War general had said before leading his men into battle, "The men from VMI will be heard from today!"

The following Monday, Lady Bird had her own day in the spotlight when she visited New York to give a speech opening a new wing of the Museum of Modern Art. She referred to her hotel suite at the Carlyle as "the tower of the Fairy Princess." It was completely glass with a view of Central Park and Manhattan and the bedroom was pink and white.

Adlai Stevenson escorted her to the museum and once there she went on a tour with the David Rockefellers, the John Rockefellers, and museum president, and the director. After dinner, she attended an artists reception in the upper gardens so she could flip a switch to the reveal the new wing.

The museum event reflects Lady Bird's life on contrasts. In a matter of days, she had been to some of the most poverty stricken areas of the nation, to VMI, and to Manhattan. That had to have been on her mind, for in her speech at the museum, she praised her generation for fighting the war on poverty and "a war against the poverty of man's spirit."

CAMPAIGN 1964 GETS UNDER WAY

Friday June 5 saw the Senator and Mrs. Bayh kicking off "Young Citizens for Johnson" in the Senate caucus room. On hand with Luci and Lynda were Charlotte Ford, daughter of Henry Ford II, Bobby Mitchell of the Washington Redskins, John Reuther, son of the labor leader, Victor Reuther, just to name a few.

President Johnson's staff had been conducting polls since the early spring of 1964. With the belief that the Republican nominee would be Barry Goldwater, the Democrats were grateful. They saw him as the easiest of all the likely opponents to beat. A July poll conducted by Lou Harris showed that the American people disagreed with Goldwater on eight out of ten issues. Despite a far right nominee and a far right Republican convention where moderates like Eisenhower and Nelson Rockefeller where heckled, Lyndon was taking nothing for granted.

The President first had to get through his own convention and pick a running mate before he could turn all of his attention toward Goldwater. Bobby Kennedy was raised as a possible running mate, and also as a potential challenger to Johnson. It was no secret that there was no love lost between Johnson and Kennedys. Bobby and Ted Kennedy turned down invitations to the May 27 State Dinner for the President of Ireland. However, the Kennedy family was represented by Mr. and Mrs. Sargent Shriver.

After day of pomp and circumstance that included a State Luncheon for the Shah of Iran and dinner with John Steinbeck, Lady Bird was hit with the stark reality of her husband's job. As she made her way through her stack of mail, she came across a letter from a lady who had lost a son in Vietnam. The mother was replying to President Johnson's letter of sympathy. Mrs. Johnson said of the letter in her diary, "Her answer was simple, dignified, and acceptant, no bitterness, which made it all the more painful." There is no doubt Lady Bird felt grief over the losses we were suffering in Vietnam.

However, her diary reflects the mood that the United States must persevere or the Communist would take advantage of any signs of weakness. When asked if she and the First Lady ever discussed Vietnam, Bess Abell said no. But, who could blame her. That was an awful chapter of American history that would we would all wish to forget. Abell does indeed have the right to keep confidential any feelings Lady Bird expressed to her.

Mrs. Johnson knew the anguish and pain her husband was going through from dealing with matters in Southeast Asia and offered her unconditional love and support. She went about her public duties and gave the commencement address at Radcliffe on June 9. Her favorite line of her remarks was, "Remember, in the most local realistic terms that education is a loan to be repaid by a gift itself." Lady Bird applauded the role women were playing in society and encouraged all the graduates to be leaders in their respective fields but not to forget their duties to their families and children.

The next day, she was delighted to join her husband at the Presidential Scholars reception. One of the President's weapons in his war on poverty was education, and he was happy to showcase some of America's brightest and youngest minds. The Johnsons personally met each student, and Lady Bird had read their biographies, and she was very pleased to see low-income students among the scholars.

For the reception, the Johnsons had invited experts from every major field. Present were Helen Hayes, Harper Lee, Alan Shepherd, Robert Oppeheimer, and Leonard Bernstein. Many of the young people didn't recognize some of the famous guest, and Lady Bird made a mental note to have name tags next time. Just another example of Mrs. Johnson wanting to make every guest at the White House feel as warm and welcome as possible.

Lady Bird hosted another one of her Women Do-ers luncheons on June 16 and invited Breathitt County Kentucky schools superintendent Marie Turner. The featured speaker was Jane Jacobs who had authored *The Death and Life of Great American Cities*. Jacobs spoke of how to keep cities from getting to impersonal and "smothering the individual." She lamented that any city can obtain funding for a beautiful park, but not for the upkeep of the park. One of the guest brought up the idea that disadvantaged and out of work youth could help maintain city parks. Lady Bird enjoyed these lunches where leading women from all over the country could discuss a problem and possible solutions.

UNTOLD GOOD AND TROUBLE

Luci's seventeenth birthday turned out to be a very momentous day in the history of the country. For on July 2, 1964, her father signed into law the Civil Rights of 1964. The act had been introduced by President Kennedy in late 1963, but it took Lyndon's legislative experience and pressure to get the act through both houses of Congress.

The 6:30 signing ceremony in the East Room received full television coverage and included all the major Congressional leaders, Mike Mansfield, Hale Boggs, and Everett Dirksen. Also on hand was Attorney General, Robert Kennedy. Lady Bird was present for the occasion and told a newswoman that it all reminded her of how Lyndon hard worked so hard to get the Civil Rights Act of 1957 passed and said this was simply "just another step in a long chain of steps." She wrote in her diary, "I left the East Room feeling that I had seen the beginning of something in this nation's history, fraught with untold good, and much pain and trouble."

She was proud that her husband, a southerner, had been the President to officially outlaw segregation, and felt that the nation was fortunate to have him at this moment in its history. For President Johnson could assist his native South in the process of desegregation.

The Johnsons headed down to the ranch shortly after the signing ceremony. They consulted with their old Texas friends about whether or not Lyndon should run. Ed Weisl told Mrs. Johnson, "Bird, I don't know any honorable way for him not to run." A. W. Moursand was crystal clear in speaking to the President. He told Johnson that as a "selfish citizen" he wanted him to run, then once elected, announce that he would just serve one term and do the best he could to help every American regardless of race or political affiliation. Once again, more evidence that Johnson was thinking of not running in 1968 long before the Vietnam War cut into his political support.

Upon their return to Washington, Lady Bird spent an afternoon in the White House and used the opportunity to catch up on her mail and contemplate her husband's future. She recorded in her diary that President Johnson was earnestly trying someway to avoid being the candidate, "But the trouble is he can't find any honorable escape."

She once again ran across more letters from families who had lost loved ones in Vietnam. "I know what an unbearable weight a great mass of those letters could be," she wrote in her diary. She was no doubt thinking of her husband's health and the burdens he must bear everyday of his life. Mrs. Johnson was worried that his heart couldn't make it through four more years of the presidency.

Throughout the summer of 1964, President Johnson carefully weighed his options for future and he consulted with Lady Bird at every turn. The day the Republicans nominated Barry Goldwater, the Johnsons only got two hours of sleep. The President woke his wife up and went over everything on his mind concerning the election, and discussed the positives and negatives of any decision he could make.

The next morning, Lady Bird was dismayed as she listened to Senator Goldwater on television. When asked about President Johnson, Goldwater answered, "Yes, I know the fellow." She thought the answer was disrespectful and hoped her husband wouldn't treat Goldwater that way.

ALL NECESSARY MEANS

July ended with the Johnsons future still an open question. However, the White House had been preparing a campaign against Goldwater. One evening, at a dinner party at the Fulbrights, Lady Bird had run into the columnist, Reston who had been at the Republican convention. When she asked him about the convention, Reston said "just one thing, work like hell."

The early days of August brought on the turning point of America's intervention in Vietnam. On Tuesday, August 4, Lady Bird noticed that McNamara, Rusk, at Bundy stayed a bit longer than usual for lunch. Also, cars kept dropping off Congressional leaders, more Cabinet officials, and the Joint Chiefs of Staff. Lady Bird soon learned the reason for all of this activity. Two navy destroyers had been attacked in the Gulf of Tonkin by North Vietnamese boats. President Johnson went on television that night to announce the attacks and the deployment of American planes as a response. Lady Bird liked the line saying that our response will be limited for "We Americans know, although others appear to forget, the risk of spreading conflicts. We still seek no wider war." He went on to ask Congress for a resolution to allow "all necessary means in support of freedom and in defense of peace in Southeast Asia."

That resolution is now known to history as the Gulf of Tonkin Resolution, and was the instrument used by President Johnson to escalate America's involvement in Vietnam. In recent years, it has been alleged that the American ships in the gulf had fired first. Indeed, some historians say convert CIA operations in Southeast Asia may have provoked attacks on the U.S. ships. Despite such conflicting reports Johnson got his resolution through both chambers of Congress, there were just two dissenting votes in the Senate. This toughness toward Vietnam served the short term political goal of blunting criticism by Goldwater that the Democrats were weak in facing the threat from communism.

DECISION TIME

Lyndon Johnson's candidacy was in doubt right up to the time of the Democratic National Convention in late August. The day before the Democrats would make their nomination official, the President told his most trusted advisor, Walter Jenkins, "I don't think a white Southerner is the man to unite this nation in this hour. I've had doubts about whether a man from where I was born, raised like I was raised, could ever satisfy the Northern Jews, Catholics, and union people." Johnson went to confide in Jenkins that he didn't think he was physically and mentally up to the task.

Jenkins and Lady Bird remained loyal to Lyndon as he toiled over his decision and offered their unconditional support to him. On August 25, Lady Bird set down and wrote her husband a letter on White House stationary and marked it personal:

Beloved—

You are as brave a man as Harry Truman—or FDR—or Lincoln. You can go on to find some peace, some achievement amidst all the pain. You have been strong, patient, determined beyond any words of mine to express.
I honor you for it. So does most of the country.
To step out now would be wrong for your country, and I can see nothing but a lonely wasteland for your future. Your friends would be frozen in embarrassed silence and your enemies jeering.
I am not afraid of *Time* or lies or losing money or defeat.
In the final analysis I can't carry any of the burdens you talked of—so I know it's only your choice. But I know you are as brave as any of the thirty-five.

I love you always
Bird

This letter to Lyndon is not surprising. Lady Bird had been long been his most trusted advisor, the one who could tell him what is really on her mind, without fear of a good dressing down by him. Lyndon did accept the nomination of the Democratic Party the day after receiving his wife's letter. As for Mrs. Johnson, she appeared at a reception with Jacqueline Kennedy during the convention that was Kennedy's only public appearance at the convention.

Many thought the President's acceptance speech mediocre at best; some even said it was the worst speech of his career. But overnight public opinion polls showed the speech had done no damage to Johnson and the convention ended on a high note. Some four thousand people attended a birthday rally and parade for Lyndon that ended with a fireworks display featuring the President's likeness. As for Lady Bird, her role was to be an avid and active campaigner for the Johnson-Humphrey ticket.

A JOURNEY OF THE HEART

During the campaign of 1960, Truman had told Lyndon there were still many people across the country that didn't know where the airport was, but they knew where the train station was. Truman said, "And if you let them know you're coming, they'll be down to listen to you." [1]

Lady Bird took Truman up on his advice and enlisted Liz Carpenter to help plan a whistle stop trip through the South. Carpenter referred to the trip as a "salvage operation" since the South had begun breaking away from the Democratic Party since President Johnson signed the Civil Rights Act. Mrs. Johnson was well aware of the tensions in her native region, but she told Carpenter, "Don't give me the easy towns, Liz. Anyone can get into Atlanta; it's the new modern South. Let me take the tough ones."

So the train made stops in Raleigh, Charleston, and Savannah, not exactly bastions of liberalism. Lady Bird is to be commended for willingly going into hostile territory and telling the South to respect the laws of the United States. The train was known as the Lady Bird Special and the trip made Mrs. Johnson a public figure in her own right.

The White House reached out to Southern political wives such as Betty Talmadge of Georgia, Lindy Boggs of Louisiana, and Carrie Davis of Tennessee for help in planning the whistle stop trip. Wife of South Carolina governor Daniel Russell, Virginia, moved into the White House for three weeks to assist Mrs. Boggs.

Liz Carpenter recalled an incident that occurred when Governor Russell invited the White House advance team to stay at the Governor's Mansion. The next morning, Russell awoke to a burning cross in the front lawn. But Mrs. Johnson held firm and made no adjustments to her trip.[2]

Carpenter held a meeting of the advance staff in the White House Mess and Mrs. Johnson made a surprise visit. She thanked them for their time and efforts and said, "I know the Civil Rights Act was right, and I don't mind saying so. But, I'm tired of people making the South the whipping boy of the Democratic Party. They are plenty of people who make snide jokes about the cornpone and red-neck." She further stated that she loved the South and was proud of it and said her and Lyndon both think the South belongs to the United States. Then she said, "For me, it is going to be a journey of the heart." Carpenter stated that Lady Bird received a standing ovation and said, "There wasn't a man there who wouldn't have gladly gone all the way Appomattox for her." [3]

Before officially announcing the 1,682 mile train trip that would cross through eight states with forty-seven stops from October 6-9, Mrs. Johnson wanted to call the governors and senators of each state to let them know she was coming. "I don't think it's courteous for a senator or governor to pick up the paper and read I'm coming to his state without hearing it first from me," she told Carpenter.

So the Friday before the trip, she sat in the West Hall for eight hours and called every governor and senator whose state she would visit. Carpenter noticed her Southern heritage rise up in her as Lady Bird talked, "Guv-nuh, this is Lady Bird." There would be a pause as they asked about Lyndon then she would say, "Fine, just fine, Guv-nuh. I'm thinking about coming to your state." Then the politician would explain the difficulties facing Democrats in the South due to civil rights. But, Mrs. Johnson kept up her Southern charm and say, "Well, I know there is a long education process that is necessary." Next, she would tell them about the Lady Bird Special and said she didn't want "the South overlooked in the campaign."

At this point her invitation would either be accepted or declined. Liz Carpenter told of two interesting reasons for regret. Senator Willis Robertson of Virginia said he would be antelope hunting and another politician said he was still grieving for his wife who had been dead for two years. Politicians being who they are more came aboard as the crowds and media attention increased as the train made its way through the South.

President Johnson couldn't make the whole trip, but he would be on hand for the sendoff in Alexandria, the halfway point in Raleigh, and for the final stop in New Orleans. Carpenter choose Raleigh since the Democratic nominee for governor, Dan Moore had brought in some conservative Democrats who were thinking about joining the Republicans. Tensions were so high that Carpenter and her advance team had to organize with the Moore and campaign and the governor separately.

The task of searching for a suitable train with a platform fit for campaigning fell to Bess Abell. Her search was fruitless, and she finally had to call President Johnson who promised to see what he could do. He found the Queen Mary, an old Pennsylvania Railroad lounge car.

Abell and her staff was able to turn the dilapidated train into a red, white, and blue hospitality car for Mrs. Johnson to greet her guest and use to make her speeches from. A speaker system was installed for the speeches and music. As the train rolled into a town either "Happy Days are Here Again" or "Hello, Lyndon" would be playing. The latter was the lyrics to "Hello, Dolly" changed to honor the President.

Abell had gathered a group of young Southern woman to serve as hostesses. They would get off the train at each stop and pass out campaign buttons and literature. Carpenter said their bright blue shirt waist dresses, white gloves, and the red, white, and blue canopy of the train combined to make "colorful cheesecake." Once two hundred and twenty-five reporters had signed up for the trip, Carpenter had to put a lid on the press pool. Thirty foreign reporters were on board the Lady Bird Special, Carpenter wrote because "there is no comparable campaign technique abroad."

President Johnson sent off the *Lady Bird Special* on the morning of October 6. Lady Bird gave a powerful speech praising the South saying, "I'm fond of the old customs—of keeping up with kinfolk, of long Sunday dinners after church, of a special brand of gentility and courtesy." She named famous Americans that hand come from the South including Thomas Jefferson and Dean Rusk. Lady Bird then told the crowd what Robert E. Lee told his men after the Civil War, "Abandon all these local animosities and raise your sons to be Americans." She was outspoken in her support of civil rights, "It would be a bottomless tragedy for our country to be racially divided. And here I want to say emphatically, this is not a challenge only in the South. It is a national challenge—in the big cities of the North as in the states of the South."

Later on in her Alexandria speech she called for the public to get involved in that effort, "I think we all understand the hard duty of assuring equal rights to all Americans falls, not only on the President of the United States, but upon all who love this land. I am sure we will rise to that duty."

Three cars served as rolling press rooms complete with Western Union and Air Express so stories could be filed on time. Helen Thomas still remembers the whistle stop tour and some of the heckling Mrs. Johnson received due to her support for the Civil Rights Act. Carpenter wrote that Mrs. Johnson told her that she was happy to be able to see the South this way and said on board the train Mrs. Johnson was glowing. She quoted Lady Bird as saying, "I love it. I'm like Briar Rabbit in the briar patch."

When President Johnson joined them in Raleigh, they had a huge downtown rally attended by gubernatorial candidate Dan Moore and his wife. Mrs. Moore was so caught up by the cheering crowds at a nighttime rally that she hugged the President and pledged her support for the Democratic ticket. Carpenter noticed that Mr. Moore "stood silently by."

As Mrs. Johnson spoke in Columbia, there were drum rolls and chants of "We want Barry!" She simply raised one hand and said, "My friends, in this country we are entitled to many viewpoints. You are entitled to yours. But, right now, I'm entitled to mine." The chants stopped and the evening news featured Mrs. Johnson's show of courage. The protest did nothing to help Goldwater and the Republican National Committee called for all protest of Mrs. Johnson to cease.

Lady Bird kept her courage up as the train rolled into the heavily black community of Orangeburg, South Carolina. Some five thousand people cheered her while trying to reach out and touch her, to thank her for her support for civil rights. She told the crowd, she wanted to visit the "land where the pavement runs out and city people don't often go."

The mayor of Charleston agreed to appear at a rally with Mrs. Johnson and some of the same protestors from Columbia were there chanting "Johnson is a communist! Johnson is a nigger lover!" However, the economic message got out as one man told Isabelle Shelton of the Washington Star that he was voting for Johnson "because I would rather stand beside a Negro in a factory than stand behind a white man in the soup line."

The mayor took Lady Bird on a carriage ride through the historic section of Charleston. She noticed signs in almost every window that read, "This house is sold on Goldwater." Once back on the train she told Carpenter, "I kept feeling like I was looking at a beautiful corpse."

The cold welcome didn't end in the Carolinas. Luci was heckled in Savannah, Georgia and said, "It seems to me that it is easy to holler a lot and make a lot of noise when you're not the one having to handle the problems." The heckling stopped and she told the young people present to not forget that one day they would be in charge and "All the emotion in the world isn't going to help…" Mrs. Johnson reached the conclusion that mentioning the protestors in speeches only helps their cause and told the speakers to simply ignore the protestors.

Congressman Boggs simply then appealed to the stomachs of Southern voters. "You know what we had on this train this morning? Hominy grits. About noontime were gonnna start servin' turnip greens and black eyed peas. Later on, further South, were gonna have some crawfish bisque, some red beans and rice and some creole gumbo." To loud cheers and applause, he would then say, "Now about this race. You're not gonna turn your back on the first Southern born president in a hundred years?" The crowd then roared, "All the way with LBJ!"

Press coverage was so positive and the crowds so huge that even the most famous segregationist of all, Governor George Wallace of Alabama saw fit to pay his respects to Lady Bird. He sent the wife of the lieutenant governor to present Mrs. Johnson with roses when the train stopped in Mobile. The First Lady was thrilled to campaign in the state where she had spent much of her childhood and still had so many relatives. She told crowds her days spent in Alabama "are filled with memories of watermelon cuttins' and pallets on the floor." When the Lady Bird Special rolled into Mississippi, both senators were on hand to welcome Mrs. Johnson.

Then came the grand finale of the whistle stop tour. President Johnson boarded the train in New Orleans and spoke to a crowd of white and blacks together cheering as he hugged his wife and kissed Luci. Both senators, Russell Long and Allen Ellender were present but Governor John McKeithen quietly stood in a corner.

Lady Bird's final speech was an appeal to the public, "We are testing as a nation whether we shall move forward with understanding of each other, and each other's needs, ever increasing out total power—economic, social, military—in common trust and faith; or whether we shall move backward, toward a denial by each of the other's needs, into a national climate of fear and distrust...But I know and I found on this trip that while the memories of the South are as old as Thomas Jefferson, their spirit is as young as Lyndon Baines Johnson."

President Johnson then declared, "I'm going to be president of all the people. And your president is going to protect the constitutional rights of every American." The crowds were cheering so wildly for the President, that Senator Ellender, no civil rights supporter, got excited and tongue tied saying, "All the way with LJB!"

Lyndon was beaming in appreciation of his wife for her successful completion of what no other First Lady had tried before. He told Carpenter, "Now, Liz that's the way to run a railroad." In the end, four of the states Lady Bird visited went to Goldwater, but historian Lewis Gould notes, "Her appearances did, however, underscore Democratic interest in the South and may have minimized defections from the party."

Looking back on the whistle stop tour, Lady Bird wrote in her diary that it was "the four most dramatic days of my political life." She further wrote that her visits were probably the closest some people would get to their government, "and I am glad we met and touched."

Lady Bird again used her influence with her husband when Walter Jenkins was arrested October 7 on a morals charge for an incident that occurred in the men's room of the YMCA. The White House received word of the incident on October 14 and Lady Bird called Mrs. Jenkins the next morning and then called her husband around noon. Mrs. Johnson wanted to offer Jenkins the number two job at KTBC and issue of statement of support for Jenkins to the press.

President Johnson advised her to be cautious, and not to make it look like they were condoning that type of behavior. But his wife held firm saying that Jenkins was one of their most loyal staff members and that if they didn't do something, "we will lose the entire love and devotion of all the people who have been with us." However, she agreed to offer Walter Jenkins the job of running the ranch and offer his family any finanicial support they needed, but Lyndon told her to do it quietly. As she got off the phone she said, "My love, my love. I pray for you, along with Walter."

Liz Carpenter then issued a statement on Mrs. Johnson's behalf, "My heart is aching today for someone who has reached the point of exhaustion in dedicated service to his country. Walter Jenkins has been carrying incredible hours and burdens since President Kennedy's assassination. He is now receiving the medical attention he needs." Coming from the First Lady's office, the statement made the issue a personal matter, not a matter of sexuality. Goldwater didn't mention the issue publicly, and the matter receding from the headlines just three days later. Furthermore, Johnson historian Robert Dallek says that even if the story had gone on longer, the resignation of Nikita Khruschev, a Chinese test of the nuclear bomb, and a Labor victory in Britain "would have eclipsed it."[4]

When the votes were counted on Election Day, President Johnson got 486 electoral votes to Goldwater's fifty-two and he won forty-four states. He received a record 43,129,484 popular votes, which was 61% of the vote, the largest margin of victory in history for a president up to that time.

Lady Bird joined her husband for a ten day vacation at the ranch after the election. Both of them certainly deserved a respite after working so hard and traveling all over the country campaigning. She held the Bible for her husband when he took the oath of office on January 20. 1965. Mrs. Johnson wrote in her diary, "My chief emotions were simply satisfaction in peoples faith in Lyndon and a renewed determination to help him use the next four years to the best of his ability and to make some steps forward."

ENDNOTES

[1] Carpenter, p. 142
[2] Carpenter, p. 146
[3] Carpnter, p. 148
[4] Dallek, p. 181

Chapter 8

BEAUTIFYING AMERICA

GREEN LEGACY FOR TOMORROW

With a whole four year term lying in front of her, Lady Bird could now decide how best to utilize the unique role she had. She was to become one of the President's top lieutenants in the War on Poverty and told friends that conservation and beautification efforts made her heart sing.

As always, Lady Bird watched from the gallery as President Johnson delivered his State of the Union address on January 4, 1965. The part of the speech that touched her was a call for preservation of American beauty to create a "green legacy for tomorrow." That sparked Mrs. Johnson to urge her husband to have Commerce Secretary Luther Hodges begin work on a Highway Beautification Bill to rid the nation's roadways of billboards and junkyards.

Regarding, beautification, Interior Secretary Stuart Udall recommended that Mrs. Johnson lead a committee to beautify Washington in order to set an example for other cities. This was a practical idea, for as a federal city, there would be no bureaucratic or institutional barriers for the committee.

Mrs. Johnson sought advice for the committee from a diverse set of people. Libby Rowe suggested in a letter to Lady Bird the same thing Udall had, to set up a special committee to beautify Washington. New York philanthropist, Mary Lasker was brought in to due to her efforts on urban beautification. Kennedy White House lawyer, Antonia Chayes advised Mrs. Johnson to focus on parts of the city often neglected by public officials.

Lady Bird met with Mr. and Mrs. Laurence Rockefeller on February 3 to discuss the President's National Conference on Beauty, which Mr. Rockefeller was to chair. Lady Bird talked to him about his passion for beautification and she expressed to him that she wanted to see results and not "a lot of words and proliferation of committees." Also, to that end when ask by Sargent Shriver to be Honorary Chair of the Head Start program, she let it be know that she wanted "to work at it." She wouldn't let anyone just use her name for a cause; she wanted to get hands on experience with the program and see the results.

Lady Bird ran into Mary Lasker that same day and she was excited about the beautification program amd Lasker said the State of the Union was the first time "a leader called for beautification of the whole country as part of his program."

Lasker was the guest speaker for Lady Bird's February 5 Women Do-ers luncheon. It was billed as the kick-off of the beautification program and Lasker made known her now infamous motto for beautification, "masses of flowers where the masses pass."

The following Monday, Lady Bird sat down in the Treaty Room with six reporters from US News and World Report. The resulting article was entitled, "Ways to Beautify American" and Mrs. Johnson was quoted as saying, "A little beauty, something that is lovely, I think can help create harmony which will lessen tensions." She also advocated regulation for billboards, "The time is ripe— the time is now—to take advantage of this yeasting, bubbling desire to beautify our cities and our countryside. I hope all Americans will join me in this effort."

And join they did. Calls and letters flooded the White House expressing support and seeking advice on ways to beautify their own communities. Public inquiries were so overwhelming that Secretary Udall brought in Sharon Francis from the Interior Department to be Mrs. Johnson's special assistant for beautification. Francis drafted letters and speeches and correspondence and helped plan beautification committee meetings and trips.

The White House was never really comfortable with the word "beautification." Liz Carpenter recalled some confusion over the word itself. When one White House aide was introduced at a party as the First Lady's beautification assistant, one girl asked, "Tell me, do you just do Mrs. Johnson's hair or do you do Lynda's and Luci's?"

Mary Lasker made good on her promise to provide "masses of flowers," cutting a check for $30,000 to line Pennsylvania Avenue with azaleas. The purchase of the 10,305 plants depleted the azalea market as far south as Houston. Lasker was not deterred. Carpenter and she went down to the National Arboretum where scientist Henry Skinner was raising thousands of azaleas. When Lasker asked him to propagate several plants for Washington, he said he didn't have the hothouses. Lasker provided the hothouses, and Skinner provided azaleas for the nation's capitol.

Plantings did raise some controversy. Yellow tulips were planted at the First Infantry Division Memorial and a veterans group wrote to Mrs. Johnson protesting that the yellow color reflected poorly on the courage of the unit. Next season, red tulips blossomed out at the memorial.

On Thursday, February 11, the Committee on Beautification held its first meeting at the White House. Mrs. Johnson had put together an impressive coalition. Present were city planners and architects including representatives from the Federal City Council, National Capitol Garden Club League, and the Committee of 100 for the Federal City. One interesting guest was the Director of Marketing for the American Petroleum Institute, Adam Rumosky. Mrs. Johnson recorded in her diary that people like Rumosky could help turn filling stations into "models of nature and I hoped they would adopt a minimum of landscaping and some excellence in design."

Lady Bird begun the meeting by reading a 1913 letter wrote by British diplomat Lord Bryce concerning a recent visit to Washington. He wrote, "You have such a chance offered to you here for building a superb capitol." She was proud to report that Norfolk was donating five hundred azalea bushes to Washington since Luci was their 1965 Azalea Queen. Secretary of Agriculture Orville Freeman sent a letter saying that his department had several hundred azaleas, magnolias, and rhododendron available.

Lady Bird presented the idea to transform the Mall into a "showcase of beauty" to be used by all Americans, and to refurbish the many squares and triangles of Washington into sources of beauty. Udall, who Lady Bird considered to be the captain of the beautification program, asked the members for suggestions and divided the group into subcommittees with specific assignments. The committee then adjourned with the charge from Mrs. Johnson "to implement what is already under way, supplement what should be under way, and to be the catalyst for action."

For the second meeting, the committee ventured out in minibuses to plant azaleas at the triangle located at Third Street in Southwest Washington. Walter Washington insisted the entourage of committee members and press visit Greenleaf Garden, a black neighborhood, where the group was greeted by two local school bands. Mrs. Johnson said a few words after encouragement at the behest of the mayor.

Mrs. Astor and Washington were voices for putting more emphasis on the black neighborhoods by providing play grounds and turning empty lots into beauty spots that could be sources of pride for the community. Astor had funded these "outdoor living rooms" for New York City and hoped to do the same for Washington, DC. Support also came from Marjorie Merriweather Post who funded landscaping for twenty schools and beautification committee member, Washington Post publisher Katherine Graham, financed the restoration of two school playgrounds.

When the Astor Foundation contributed $400,000 for outdoor living room for Buchanan School in a poor area of Washington, Mrs. Johnson said, "Who can put a price tag on boredom? Who can add up the cost of unchallenged energies? Schoolyards simply cannot be locked up at 3 pm each day. They must be transformed into round-the-clock community playgrounds as an answer to urban problems." Therein lays the intersection of the beautification program with the War on Poverty. Urban renewal projects gave new hope to those living in low income areas and made children happy to come to school every day since they had new playgrounds. As Mrs. Johnson told Secretary Udall shortly after the March 9 meeting, "All of our efforts will fail unless people in these neighborhoods can see the challenge and do the work on their own front yards." Indeed Lady Bird would occasionally ride around the low income areas of Washington in an unmarked car and notice less broken windows in areas that the committee had sponsored outdoor living rooms or play ground restorations.

Liz Carpenter realized that beautification was striking a nerve when members of Congress began to solicit the White House for letters of support for local projects or for an appearance of the First Lady at a dedication ceremony. Carpenter wrote, "Even Senator Everett Dirksen, Republican leader, wanted Mrs. Johnson to come see newly refurbished downtown Peoria!" President Johnson didn't hesitate in telling his wife to go. One Republican Congressman commented, "Mrs. Johnson has done so much for beautification that I feel guilty every time I plant a geranium." However, Lady Bird went out of her way to make beautification a bipartisan issue because all Americans should take pride in the appearance of their country. As she said, "our challenge is to fight ugliness in a nation where there is great freedom of action or inaction for every individual and interest, and where there is virtually no artistic control."

GREAT ADVENTURES

Part of Mrs. Johnson's beautification efforts was to encourage Americans to get out and explore their own country in her "Discover America" tours. Years later, Helen Thomas recalled those trips as "great adventures."

The genesis of the "Discover America" movement was a visit to Snake River in Wyoming's Grand Teton National Park on August 16, 1964. The rain was pouring down so hard, that tarps had to be used to keep Lady Bird and the other rafters dry. Carpenter wrote the purpose of the trip was "to show how nature unmolested by signs was more beautiful." Humorist Art Buchwald was along on this trip and made jokes with the purpose of the trip. Passing by beautiful meadows and snow-capped mountains he would say, "What a lovely place for a lot of billboards."

While on the Grand Teton trip, Lady Bird became the first presidential wife to visit an Indian Reservation. Also, she spoke at the University of Utah and challenged all Americans to join her in the conservation movement saying we "can never remove the slums or the prejudices, or the ugliness, unless citizens join in the great adventure of our time." When she dedicated Flaming Gorge Dam she said, "Enjoy the beauty of your hills and protect it for your children."

Secretary of Interior, Mo Udall was along on this trip, and it allowed he and Mrs. Johnson to discuss conservation and build a relationship that would enable both of them to work together during her tenure in office. Indeed, Udall gave President Johnson a glowing report on Lady Bird's Western tour, "Mrs. Johnson was extremely effective on her 'land and people' tour in the West last week." He further stated her passion for nature and conservation" have a national impact that is the finest kind of presidential politics.

Liz Carpenter and Lady Bird's staff organized a trip to Big Bend National Park in April 1966. Located in Texas, the 708,000 acre park was the most remote in the national park system, two-hundred and fifty miles away from the nearest town.

Getting to the park involved flying to San Antonio, then transferring to a smaller plane that would fly four-hundred miles to an abandon World War II airstrip. Once on the ground, Johnson and her entourage had to take an eighty mile bus trip to the park entrance where a southwestern lunch of barbecue, frijoles, and slaw was served. Then, it was another fifteen miles to the hotel. Carpenter said all you could see was "land, land land," and she quoted Mrs. Johnson as saying, "It's the part of the world that was left over when the Lord made it."

Johnson and her party explored as much as the heavenly leftovers as they could. Her and Secretary of the Interior, Mo Udall made their way along the three mile "Lost Mine Trial" followed by eighty-five reporters and proceeded by photographers angling to get the perfect picture. However, getting press coverage for the Big Bend trip was no small feat. Eighty miles of telephone wire stretched to Alpine, Texas and film had to be airlifted out to meet the East Coast deadlines. Carpenter recalled how an assistant to Udall put a donkey outside the press room wearing a sign on his pike that said, "Pony Express wire service copy here."

After an evening, of sitting around the fire telling stories about the old West, Lady Bird and her party awoke to a breakfast of flapjacks and ham provided by the Odessa Chuck Wagon Gang. The First Lady planted a pinion tree on a site where the park service was putting up a concession. Everyone then made their way down to the Rio Grande where twenty-four rafts awaited to take Johnson and her entourage down eleven miles of the famous river. In her diary Mrs. Johnson wrote, "it seemed like fifty miles." But she enjoyed seeing the towering cliffs and mountains of Big Bend and showing the scenery off to the nation.

The group stopped for lunch at a sandbar that Carpenter named "Rattlesnake Bar." Mrs. Johnson wondered how they were able to get the portable toilets up the mountain ahead of them. Such accommodations provoked Carpenter to say that, "Frankly, I like the parks where all the concessions are run by the Rockefellers."

So Carpenter was pleased when the group got to Rio Grande Village Campground where a lunch of stakes and Margaritas awaited them. The Big Bend leg of the "Discover America" tour had been a success, the following week after Mrs. Johnson's trip, park attendance tripled.

LADY BIRD'S BILL

Right before the election of 1964, the Johnson Administration got its first major legislative victory in its conservation campaign. President Johnson signed into law the Wilderness Act on September 3, 1964. The act resulted in the addition of seven million acres to the National Wilderness Preservation System.

The following year, Mrs. Johnson and her staff fought hard against the billboard lobby to get Congress to pass the Highway Beautification Act of 1965. Except for Vermont and Hawaii, most states had little or no regulation of billboards. Historian Lou Gould notes that local communities could require companies to remove billboards but said the "industry with its timely contributions to candidates and campaigns as the 1950s ended" created little incentive to enforce the law. The extent of Congressional control of billboards was to grant states an extra half a percent of funding if they regulated billboards.

As a Senator, President Johnson was sympathetic to the advertising industry. He opposed the extra half percent funding and supported legislation that exempted land zoned for business purposes from funding restrictions. Johnson was even recognized by the Outdoor Advertising Association of Texas for being "most helpful in the passage of this act and for being consistently opposed to this trampling of people's rights."

By the time Johnson became president, public opinion was beginning to drift toward support for stricter billboard regulations. Potter Bend came out with his book in 1964, *God's Own Junkyard* that was outspoken in its support for regulation, "There are presently some 800,000 miles of federally aided highways in the United States and the billboard lobby is permitted to deface every blessed mile of them."

Lady Bird noticed the eyesores that junkyards and billboards were on her yearly drives from Texas to Washington when her husband was in Congress. Just before the election of 1964, President Johnson's Natural Beauty Task Force called for stricter regulation of billboards and suggested the raising of the half percent bonus to two percent as well as the creation of service areas along the highways where no billboards were to be allowed. So both of the Johnsons envisioned billboard and junkyard regulation of some kind by the time 1965 came along.

Indeed, in late November 1964, President Johnson called Secretary of Commerce Luther Hodges with the news, "Lady Bird wants to know what you're going to do about all those junkyards along the highways?" That set into motion the entire bureaucracies of the Commerce Department and the White House to work finding possible methods to regulate billboards.

The task would not be easy. A report from the Bureau of Public Roads found that there were 16,000 junkyards along the interstate system that the federal government had the authority to regulate. Naturally, the most difficult task would be battling with the advertising industry to regulate billboards. The Commerce Department recommended extended the 1958 highway bill to equate state highway funding with the states efforts to regulate billboards and junkyards.

White House lobbying efforts were lead by Bill Moyers, who by the spring of 1965 hand worked out an agreement with Phillip Tocker, a lobbyist for the Outdoor Advertising Association of America (OAAA). The deal allowed billboards in commercial and industrial areas if the OAAA would agree to a ban of billboards from the scenic areas of interstates and federally funded primary road systems.

President Johnson mentioned highways in his 1965 State of the Union address saying, "a new and substantial effort must be made to landscape highways to provide places of relaxation and recreation wherever our roads run." Moreover, Lady Bird mentioned her intentions regarding highways telling *US News and World Report*, "public feeling is going to bring about regulation, so that you don't have a solid diet of billboards on the roads." Letters went out from her office that advocated "the elimination of unsightly billboards."

Just in time for the White House Conference on Natural Beauty, administration and billboard industry representatives agreed on a bill. The industry agreed to a ban of billboards except in commercial and industrial areas. However, that created a loophole for the advertising industry. That is, they could simply get local and state government to change zoning laws to allow billboards.

Not everyone was happy with the compromise. The final bill went to Congress on May 27, 1965 without the support of environmental groups such as garden clubs because President Johnson called for billboards and junkyards to be banned "except in those areas of commercial and industrial use." So, "Lady Bird's Bill" landed on Capitol Hill with no grassroots support from anti-billboard groups and lack of support from rural billboard owners, the tourism industry, and politicians whose campaigns relied on support from the local billboard industry.

The White House put all its political muscle behind passing the Highway Beautification Bill. Lady Bird got involved with legislation in a manner in which no First Lady had been involved before. She worked closely with the administration legislative liaison, Lawrence O' Brien to track the bill, and worked with him to drop portions of the bill that Congresss didn't support.

Lady Bird's efforts for the legislation begin in earnest on September 11 when she sat in on a strategy session with key Johnson aides. Historian Lou Gould noted "Not even Eleanor Roosevelt had sat in on such meetings, nor had she been giving assignments to woo votes in Congress."[1] By the time of this meeting, the White House had altered the bill to give the Secretary of Commerce more leverage in billboard regulation. The meeting ended with Mrs. Johnson assigned to four Congressmen to call and solicit votes for the legislation. One of her assigned members was Illinois Congressman John Kluczynski, a chairman of subcommittee crucial to the bill. Her call was a success for a White House aide said, "the Congressman is all for anything we want."

On September 16, the Senate passed the bill but it required the government to compensate billboard owners who had their signs removed. By this time, the administration was making concessions to get any type of highway beautification bill before Congress. And who can blame them? In politics, you don't always get you want, you have to be willing to compromise, especially when facing a powerful lobby such as the advertising industry. Now all sites were set on the House.

The bill cleared the House Public Works Committee just five days after the Senate passage. The administration knew they had a fight on their hands when the Highway Beautification Bill passed the House Rules committee by just 7-6. Liz Carpenter went lobbying for the bill herself to Texas Congressmen that she knew. She wrote, "I put on my best perfume and went to Capitol Hill." She urged Harold Coolidge, a cousin of President Coolidge to urge Republicans to vote for the bill.

Carpenter ran across Kansas Republican Congressman Chester Mize one evening at a dinner party and urged him to vote for the Highway Beautification Bill. He told her, that he really didn't know anyone at the White House to call on when he needed something. Carpenter told Mize that he could always call her.

The very next morning, Mize called and asked Carpenter if she could arrange a tour of the White House for some nuns from Kansas. The nuns were very pleased and Mize told Carpenter that he would do what he could to support the bill. However, when the time came, Mize vote no.

October saw the final push for the bill. President Johnson was quoted as saying, "You know I love that woman and she wants that Highway Beautification Bill", and added. "by God, were going to get it for her." Mrs. Johnson tried to ease any fears the anti-billboard lobby had about the bill by saying, "it is a reasonable regulation, and thus is a major stride toward achieving the goal of beauty along our highways to which we all aspire."

Once the voting reached the House floor, Republicans publicly showed contempt for both of the Johnsons. Republican Congressman Melvin Laird said "we must pass this tonight so that it can be delivered to the lovely first lady as a present or package. . ." Bob Dole, then a young Congressman, went as far as to introduce an amendment to replace the words "Secretary of Commerce" with "Lady Bird" in the text of the bill. The measure failed by a voice vote.

Final passage through Congress was finally achieved on October 13 and President Johnson signed the measure into law on October 22. Upon signing the President said, "The law will bring the wonders of nature back into our lives." The bill was not perfect, but it was the only legislation that the Congress could agree upon. Pictures show Mrs. Johnson beaming as her husband presented her with one of the pens used to sign the bill. Passage of the Highway Beautification Act raised Mrs. Johnson's profile as an activist First Lady and it brought her some criticism.

The head of the Dallas Outdoor Advertising Company wrote President Johnson, "The legislation is a whim of Mrs. Johnson and you are backing it to the hilt with no regard to the effect it will have on thousands of people in the outdoor advertising business." A billboard appeared for a short time in Montana calling for the impeachment of Lady Bird. She laughed it all of by saying, "Imagine me keeping company with Chief Justice Warren!"[2] The Chief Justice of the Supreme Court is the prosiding office at impeachment trials.

Lady Bird was more involved with the implementation phase of the highway beautification bill than she was with the actual passage through Congress. From the beginning, outdoor advertising interest sought to limit the power of the Secretary of Commerce to regulate billboards. Mrs. Johnson and her staff paid close attention to how the Commerce Department was writing and enforcing regulations. Despite the fact that funding for billboards was not including in the 1966 highway bill, Lady Bird remained just as committed to her cause throughout 1967. Work did continue on highway beautification as the Bureau of Public Roads created the possession of Coordinator of Highway Beauty.

Congressional support for funding highway beautification waned as the cost of Vietnam increased. Congress did provide some funding in the 1967 highway bill, but the Federal Highway Act of 1968 lowered that funding.

As her time in office came to and end, Lady Bird extended highway beautification by calling for new road construction projects to avoid destroying parks and historic places. She told the American Road Builders at their 1966 convention, "What a tragedy it would be if we do not make our highways instruments of beauty as well as convenience in the vast construction program which lies ahead of us." Of her efforts Lou Gould noted, "Lady Bird could only set an example for policymakers and serve as a rallying point for citizens concerned about proliferating highways."[3]

Once leaving office, she kept up her efforts to beautify the highways. She begin in 1969 to sponsor beautification awards for employees of the Texas Highway Department. The awards are presented annually at the LBJ state park in Stonewall, Texas. She said of the award in 1980 that it "helped to make preservation and propagations of our natural assets an ongoing aim—happening naturally in the course of a days work."

It can be said that it was Lady Bird, who as the turmoil of the 1960s drew on that kept the focus of the Congress, President, and country on highway beautification. Her labor of love for the scenic beauty of America did provide some results. The Department of Transportation reported in 1979 that 1,055 illegal junkyards had been shut down and another 2,300 had been screened or removed. Flaws remained, however, as there were still nearly 11,000 illegal junkyards left.[4] Still, Mrs. Johnson's efforts made highway beautification a part of the public policy debate for decades.

ENDNOTES

[1] Lewis L. Gould, *Lady Bird Johnson: Our Environmental First Lady* (University Press of Kansas, 1999) pp. 96-97
[2] Gould, p. 101-102
[3] Gould, p. 106
[4] Gould, p. 107

Chapter 9

SEARCHING FOR A WAY OUT

WHITE HOUSE WEDDING

Lyndon and Lady Bird's time was not all consumed by important policy matters such as highway beautification, remember, they were parent also. It was during Lyndon's term in office when Lucy and Lynda both got married. Lucy caused quite a stir by changing the spelling of her name to L-U-C-I when she turned sixteen. Her mother didn't mind for she wrote in her diary, "There is quite a flap these days as to which way it's spelled. As for me, why should I object so mightily if my L-U-C-Y chooses to spell it another way? I remember when I was about fourteen; I spelled my middle named Byrd, after I had given up ever managing to be called Claudia!"

Lady Bird wasn't so accepting when Luci made another change in her life. She had been attending Catholic mass since the age of thirteen, and on her eighteenth birthday, she officially was confirmed into the Catholic Church. It was such a disappointment to Luci's Protestant family. However, both her parents and her sister Lynda attended the July 2, 1965 baptism service at St. Matthews Cathedral, where JFK's funeral had been. That coincidence made Lady Bird uneasy about the whole affair, and she wrote in her diary that she wasn't happy but, "Maybe her earnest search is at an end, because it always had been a search." After the ceremony, Luci went to confession and Lynda left in tears prompting Lady Bird to write, "I could not help but think we went in four and come out three."

Luci was about to drop another surprise on her parents and the country. Around 11:30 on Christmas Eve night of 1965, Liz Carpenter received a call from Luci, who was at the ranch. Her boyfriend Patrick Nugent had just giving her an engagement ring, and Luci wanted it announced to the media before Midnight Mass. Liz was able to release the news that "The President and Mrs. Lyndon Baines Johnson tonight announced the engagement of their daughter, Luci Baines to Patrick John Nugent of Waukegan, Illinois."[1] Thus the first White House wedding in fifty years was set into motion.

Carpenter battled the press every step of the way to keep the bridal dress design a secret, Luci didn't want Patrick to see the dress until their wedding day. Liz won out in the end, but problems kept cropping up. She had a difficult time searching for St. Agatha, the patron saint of nursing so Luci could lay a bouquet at her feet after the wedding. Bess Abell and Carpenter had to have the National Gallery of Art both paint a portrait of St. Agatha and sculpt a bronze statue. With that problem out of the way, the wedding dress then became a political issue.

Word reached David Dubinksy of the International Ladies'Garment Workers Union that the maker of Luci's dress, Priscilla of Boston, was non-union. Carpenter wrote that Dubinsky "literally wept over the phone when confronted with the thought" that President Johnson would allow his daughter to wear a dress not made by union hands. A compromise was reached when Priscilla agreed to have the dress assembled at a union shop. Labor issues arose once again when Carpenter borrowed blowers from United Airlines to help air condition the Shrine of the Immaculate Conception on the wedding day since the blowers were not in use due to a strike. Carpenter was happy, as the weather was forecasted to be up in the 90s on the day on the wedding day. Secretary of Labor Willard Wirtz told Carpenter, "No! No! I know it's tough, but this strike affects 35,000 men. Feelings are high. Negotiations are difficult. All we need is a struck airline truck photographed at the President's daughter's wedding. Call them off!" So, the wedding guest had to sit and sweat. Lady Bird wrote in her diary that she was so hot that she prayed for the August 6, 1966 ceremony to be over soon, and Lynda almost fainted in the heat.

After a White House reception, Luci gave Carpenter a gold bracelet engraved with the message, "For immediate realease, I'm grateful to Liz. LJN 8/6/66/" The marriage produce a child, Patrick Lyndon, who was born on June 25, 1967.

Lynda had been courting a twenty-eight year old Marine named Charles "Chuck" Robb who was on the White House Color Guard. Robb was headed for Vietnam in April of 1968, so the coupled settled on a December 9, 1967 White House wedding. Robb was, like Lynda, an Episcopalian, so Carpenter was thankful to not have to get involved in "a complicated Church in the midst of ecumenical indecisions. . ."[2] Union designers Geoffrey Beane and Cyril Magnin handled the wedding dress and air conditioning was not an issue in December, so this wedding went off much simpler. However, that didn't stop some five hundred reporters from covering the event. While Carpenter was battling the press, Bess Abell was politely declining request for invitations, even from a leading Washington hostess who called the White House literally crying to be invited.

The White House wedding was a success and Lady Bird wrote, "My heart was a roaring tumult of pride, of desire to wring from this wonderful time every second of pleasure, living to the fullest this milestone of their lives." Canon McAllister of Lady Bird's St. Barnabas Church of Fredericksburg, Texas officiated the ceremony. Chuck, Lynda, President Johnson, Lady Bird, and Chuck's parents received the 640 guest in the Blue Room and refreshments were served in the State Dining Room and in a pink tent that was set up for the occasion. Among the Robb and Johnson relatives were Vice President and Mrs. Humphrey, the Chief Justice and Mrs. Earl Warren, every member of the Cabinet, as well as Theodore Roosevelt's 83 year old daughter, Alice Roosevelt Longworth. Liz Carpenter and Bess Abell were glad to have both daughters married off and the trouble of planning White House weddings a distant memory.

GUESS WHO CAME TO LUNCH

As 1967 and 1968 went on, the situation in Vietnam worsened to the point where President Johnson's approval ratings were at all time lows and no member of the Johnson family could not make public appearances without protestors showing up and hecklers stood in front of the White House yelling, "Hey, hey, LBJ how many kids have you killed today?" Years later Luci would recall sitting in the White House crying while listening to that chant, knowing that her father had much at stake in the war, since both son-in-laws were fighting in the Vietnam.

With all that in mind Lady Bird wrote in her diary in 1967, "I don't know how we can endure another four-year term in the presidency." Due to Lyndon's health and the war, it was decided in late summer of 1967 that he would not run for another term. The president took his time in deciding a proper time to announce that he was retiring from politics.

As the President was contemplating his future, Lady Bird went on with her official duties and hosted a Women Doers lunch on January 18, 1968 that was to focus on crime. Singer and actress Eartha Kitt was invited upon the recommendation of Sharon Francis and Liz Carpenter since Kitt had testified to Congress in favor of the President's anti-crime legislation. When President Johnson entered the room, Kitt confronted him, "Mr. President, what do you do about delinquent parents—those who have to work and are too busy too look after their children?" He told her that Social Security legislation was just passed that provided millions of dollars for day care centers. Kitt was not pleased but Lyndon told her that those were issues for the women to discuss at the lunch.

During the question period Kitt stood up and confronted Lady Bird, "Boys I know across the nation feel it doesn't pay to be a good guy." She moved into closer to the First Lady and said that boys don't want to behave for fear of being sent to Vietnam saying, "You are a mother, too, although you have had daughters and not sons. I am a mother and I know the feeling of having a baby come out of my guts. I have a baby and then you send him off to war. No wonder the kids rebel and take pot. And. Mrs. Johnson, in case you don't understand the lingo, that's marijuana!"

Lady Bird was proud to match her stare for stare and Sharon Francis said she sat ready to jump up in between Mrs. Johnson and Kitt, since Francis was closer than the Secret Service. After Kitt finished her tirade, Betty Hughes, wife of the New Jersey governor, rose to her feet and recalled how she had lost a husband in World Ward II and had sons in Vietnam and said, "I think that anybody who takes pot because there is a war on is a kook. These young people are still juniors. They have to be regulated. I hope we adults are still in control." After the wife of the Washington Mayor, Bennetta Washington, who, like Kitt was African-American, stood up and said we must channel our anger in constructive manners, Lady Bird spoke:

"Because there is a war on, and I pray that there will be a just and honest peace—that still doesn't give us a free ticket not to try to work for better things—against crime in the streets, and for better education and health for our people. I cannot identify as much as I should. I have not lived the background that you have, nor can I speak as passionately or as well, but we must keep our eyes and our hearts and our energies fixed on constructive areas and try to do something that will make this a happier, better-educated land." The room broke into applause. Kitt's confrontations with Mrs. Johnson lead to a slow decline of her career and she told *Newsweek* shortly after the luncheon, "if Mrs. Johnson was embarrassed, that's her problem."[3]

THE ONLY WAY OUT

A few weeks after the now famous Kitt luncheon, Lynda and Lady Bird hosted wounded Vietnam Veterans from Walter Reed and Bethesda hospital to a pizza party in the White House theater on February 7. Lynda had been visiting both hospitals under cover until the media was tipped, so Lady Bird felt the need to host this private party for the veterans. Mrs. Johnson was moved as she greeted the guest as some were amputees and confined to wheelchairs. The First Lady spent ten minutes at each table and was thrilled to learn that the first veteran she talked to was from Austin. This event brought her to face to face with the consequences of her husband's policies, and she felt some regret at seeing those fine young me having to live the rest of their lives in their current conditions.

Senators Robert Kennedy and Eugene McCarthy were giving President Johnson a stiff challenge in the Democratic primaries, mostly due to Vietnam. Lyndon realized the he lacked the political support to change his mind and seek re-election. More and more he was telling Lady Bird, "I do not believe I can unite this country." So, on the evening of March 31, 1968, President Johnson announced that he would not be running again saying, " I do not believe that I should devote an hour or a day of my time to any personal partisan causes or to any duties other than the awesome duties of this office—the Presidency of your country." Johnson felt like he could not enter peace talks with North Vietnam as a political candidate; for they would just think he was negotiating for the short term political benefits, not for the good of the Vietnamese people. Lady Bird ended her diary entry for that day, "Lyndon's speech had been, I believe, nobly done, and in its way almost as dramatic as our entrance into this job…" The statement she had Carpenter issue to the press was simple and straightforward, "We have done a lot; there's a lot left to do in the remaining months; maybe this is the only way to get it done."

THE LAST HURRAH

Lady Bird continued her beautification and Discover American initiatives those last few months she had in office. She led thirty-eight foreign reporters on a Discover America tour of Texas and she enjoyed showing off the landscape of her home state to the foreign press. Press coverage of this trip was overshadowed by the assassination of Martin Luther King and Lady Bird was happy to get out of Washington which was locked down by the National Guard due to riots. She took the foreign press to Fredericksburg, the LBJ Ranch, Johnson City, San Antonio, Padre Island, and the Hill Country. On the last day the reporters sang "Auld Lang Syne" to Mrs. Johnson, which seemed fitting for one of her final trips as First Lady.

In June, Lady Bird went to Oregon where she hosted a beef fondue supper at Timberline Lodge, which hand been handmade during the New Deal by the Civilian Conservation Corps. A campfire followed with folksongs and speakers telling the history and Indian lore of Oregon. Mrs. Johnson and her party then went to the Columbia River Gorge and Bonneville Dam. That same month, Bobby Kennedy was assassinated and the Johnsons went to his funeral in New York on June 8. Lady Bird met with Bobby's widow, Ethel Kennedy, and Mrs. Kennedy thanked her for being there. Also at the funeral, Lady Bird and Jacqueline Kennedy just exchanged glances but several days latter Kennedy sent Lady Bird a note, "Sometimes there are no words to say things—only this—I am deeply grateful."

Secretary of the Interior Udall called Sharon Francis on August 2 and recommended that Lady Bird make one last trip. It soon was called "The Last Hurrah" by Liz Carpenter and Sharon Francis. Udall wished to have the trip focused on helping Democrats with the 1968 campaign but have a beautification theme. However, Lady Bird wished to have this trip after the election so it would not have any political tints to it. This trip took Lady Bird from Cape Kennedy in Florida to the Redwood Forest in California. Mrs. Johnson was extremely pleased when her husband singed into a law an act creating the Redwoods Park. Upon signing the bill he said his wife is an "enthusiastic, tenacious, pugnacious, persistent advocate of conservation every hour in this house."[4]

On November 12, Lady Bird was presented a plaque presented by Laurence Rockefeller on behalf of the National Recreation and Park Association. Then she joined her Beautification Committee at the Department of Interior for special going away gift presentations. The 1965 Inaugural Committee provided 220 dogwood trees for Columbian Island located near the National Airport. Next, The Society for a More Beautiful National Capital provided one million daffodils and 2,500 dogwoods. All this was intended for the island, and then Mrs. Johnson got a pleasant surprise. Secretary Udall announced that Columbia Island was being renamed "Lady Bird Johnson" park. She was also named to the Advisory Board of the National Park Service and they drove Lady Bird by the park being named in her honor. She wrote her diary of the occasion, "there was a slightly mournful feeling that the end of our beautification effort—together, at least—was about to take place."

December saw Lady Bird having her final meeting of the Committee for the Preservation of the White House in the Yellow Room on the 12th. The committee was provided a list of the acquisitions of the White House collection since Lady Bird took office and they were taking on a tour of the White House to view the additions to the collection.

Lady Bird then met with the next First Lady, Pat Nixon. She took Mrs. Nixon on a tour of the White House residence to show them the bedrooms and living areas they would be using. Nixon asked how much furniture was available at the warehouse and how much money she would have to redo the private areas with.

Mrs. Johnson told her that there would enough money to "make their bedrooms and the West Hall seem like home."

Lady Bird herself was about to return home to Texas and was looking forward to the years of rest and thought of a favorite line in *India's Love Lyrics*, "I seek, to celebrate my glad release, the Tents of Silence and the Camp of Peace." On the morning of January 20, Inauguration Day, Lady Bird went into the Yellow Room and Lincoln Sitting Room to "absorb the feeling" of those rooms in the family residence in which she had made some many memories those past few years. Clark and Mary Clifford hosted a farewell lunch for them at their Washington home that included most of their White House staff and Texas friends. Several days before, Bess Abell was riding out of the White House gates with Lady Bird and asked her if she would miss it. To which Lady Bird answered, "Oh yes, I'll miss it every day, I'll miss it like a front tooth. But you know there is absolutely nothing in the world that would make me willing to pay the price for another ticket of admission."[5]

Not that loyal, staff, friends, and supporters would let the Johnsons quietly leave public life. A crow awaited them at Andrews Air Force Base as a band played "Hail to the Chief," "Yellow Rose of Texas," and the sentimental classic fit for the occasion, "Auld Lang Sine." There was even a twenty-one gun salute. Staff and friends of the Johnson said there last farewell, and they were soon aboard *Air Force One* bound for home. Once the plane landed at Bergstrom Air Force Base in Texas, a five thousand strong crowd awaited them including the lieutenant governor and The Long Horn Band which played "Hail to the Chief." Lyndon told the crowd, "Whether we are Democrats or Republicans, Texans, or New Yorkers, we love our country, or we ought to love it."

The Johnson family then took a small plane to the ranch where yet another crowd awaited them. Some five hundred locals that were old friends of Lyndon and Lady Bird had showed up at the ranch hangar to welcome them back home. Lyndon gave a long speech telling the crowd how much he was glad to be back home to Texas. Once inside the house, Lady Bird noticed the luggage piled high just inside the kitchen door. Long gone were the days of everything small detail of her life taken care of. She wrote in her diary, "It would be some time before we get to the bottom of that stack."

PRESIDENT OF THE RANCH

Lyndon Johnson slipped into periods of depression now that he no longer held power or was close to the center of power, especially since the Republicans were now in control of the White House. He begins to eat whatever he wanted and find comfort in drinking. Lady Bird had a calming effect on him, and he wanted her by his side every minute, or at least knows of her whereabouts and when she would return to the ranch.

Lady Bird would go shopping for clothes and come back and model them for Lyndon who picked out what he liked. He did the same for Luci, Lynda, and his secretaries, having clothes sent to the ranch and choosing what he thought looked best. Johnson went riding around the ranch in his Lincoln convertible and let the foreman know if a fence were broken of if there was a stray cow. The man who had once been President of the United States was now president of a ranch.

Lyndon did spend some time writing his memoirs, creating the LBJ Foundation, designing his library, and founding the Lyndon Baines Johnson School of Public Affairs at the University of Texas at Austin. He was like a proud new father on May 22, 1971, the day he officially opened and dedicated the LBJ Library in Austin. President Nixon, former Vice President Humphrey, and Barry Goldwater where all present as Johnson declared, "It's all here, the story of our time—with the bark off."

At the urging of her husband, Lady Bird accepted a seat on the board of regents at the University of Texas from then Texas governor Preston Smith in 1970. Lyndon had a major heart attack in June 1972 while visiting Lynda in Virginia. He survived, but he had to use portable oxygen as chest pains became more and more frequent. Lady Bird left the ranch on January 22, 1973 for a board of regents meeting. Around four in the afternoon, Secret Service Agent Mike Howard heard Lyndon's voice on his radio, "One to Mike! Get me Mike." Howard went to Lyndon's bedroom and found the former president unconscious on the floor. He was then airlifted to San Antonio where he was pronounced dead at 4:35 in the afternoon. Lady Bird was rushed out of her regents meeting and got on a helicopter to San Antonio. Howard told her what had happened and she said, "Well, we expected it, didn't we?" Lyndon lay in state at the LBJ Library, the U. S. Capitol Rotunda, and had a full state funeral in Washington. He was buried at the Johnson family cemetery at the ranch.

ON HER OWN

Lady Bird has since carried on, and still remains very much involved in beautification. She planted wildflowers on pastures at the ranch where Lyndon wouldn't let her before. Lady Bird lamented that once lovely Austin was getting